Jadoussac

Lawrence

Manoir
Richelieu

Murray Bay

St.

Isle Aux C

River

sle d'Orleans

J.M. 1930

SAGUENAY
(SÂGINAWA)
River of Deep Waters

The frowning but magnificent
heights along the Saguenay.

SAGUENAY
"SÂGINAWA"
The River of Deep Waters

by BLODWEN DAVIES

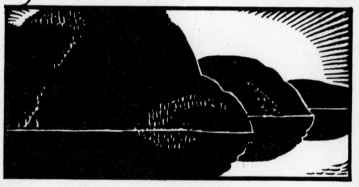

with illustrations by
Paul Caron & G. A. Cuthbertson

McClelland & Stewart, Limited
Publishers   ɤ   Toronto

CONTENTS

5

ILLUSTRATIONS

I

THE ST. LAWRENCE

IF THERE is a river anywhere haunted by old ships and old adventurers, surely it must be the St. Lawrence. I am quite sure that there are still summer nights when ears delicately attuned to the things of long ago may hear the sweep and splash of Viking oars, or late sunsets when they catch the rustle of Basque sails, lowering for the night. There is no doubt whatever that there are still echoes of the old songs of Normandy and Brittany as they were sung from sea-washed decks, and even lusty tunes that came from Devon with Saunders' sea dogs. And shrill among kindlier echoes are the savage war whoops of exultant red warriors paddling their slim canoes homeward at the end of a raid upon their foes.

Of all Canada, the lands lying on the shores of the St. Lawrence are the most characteristic. Nowhere in the world can these river-born towns and cities be duplicated, for they are the essence of the spirit of this great river.

On many counts the St. Lawrence can claim to be exceptional. Its very volume is overwhelming, its beauty full of variety and surprises, its traditions romantic and inspiring. Ships may travel a thousand miles eastward and a thousand miles westward and still be upon the tributary waters of the St. Lawrence. Montreal is a seaport, and one of the greatest in the world, yet it is on an island in the St. Lawrence, far far beyond even the salty perfume of the sea. The river thrusts itself like a spear head far into the continent, with Montreal upon its tip.

In *All Afloat*, a chronicle of the waterways of Canada, Colonel William Wood, whose ancestors have known the St. Lawrence for generations past, writes of the river with a proper pride.

"The St. Lawrence basin," he says, "by itself is a thing to marvel at for its mere stupendous size alone. Its mouth and estuary are both so vast that their salt waters far exceed that of all other river systems put together. Its tide runs farther in from the Atlantic than any other tide from this or any other ocean. And its 'Great Lakes' are appropriately known by their proud name because they contain more fresh water than all the world beside. Size for size, this one river system is so pre-eminently first in the sum of these

Lake steamers at anchor
below Montreal.

11

three attributes that there is no competing second to be found elsewhere. . . . Nature laid out the St. Lawrence Basin so that it not only led into the heart of the continent but connected with every other system from the Atlantic to the Pacific and from the Tropics to the Polar Sea. Little by little the pioneers found out that they could paddle and portage the same canoe, by inland routes, many thousands of miles to all four points of the compass: eastward to the Atlantic between the Bay of Fundy and New York; westward till, by extraordinary effort, they passed up the giant Saskatchewan and through the mighty ranges that look upon the Pacific; southward to the Mississippi and the Gulf of Mexico; northward to Hudson Bay or down the Mackenzie to the Arctic Ocean."

Here from the shores of the St. Lawrence went the discoverers of the continent, La Salle, Du Lhut, Marquette, La Vérendrye and their kindred spirits.

The river has a personality and it has impressed itself upon its people. The Valley has been the cradle of the Canadian people, a kind nesting place for those who, in pioneer days, had the courage to cross the sea to new and untried lands, or those who sacrificed everything but their souls to the principle of loyalty in the revolution of the American colonies, and trekked north to

13

live under the flag to which they had been born. More than a dozen generations have used the broad river as a highway to adventure, and from the metropolis to the tiniest hamlet that clusters in the fold of a hill each and all have taken on something of their character from the river.

The St. Lawrence can be hauntingly beautiful and you may come upon it in many moods. The harbor of Montreal at dusk, when the day's business is done and serenity descends upon the deserted docks, is something to remember. Slowly the river turns a dusky blue grey and miles of yellow lights wink along the quays, their reflections lying like golden fringe upon the uneasy water, still restless with the labors of the day. Or, out where the water broadens between the sloping banks and ribbon-like farmlands, you will find the river lying drowsily under a summer sun, gleaming and wincing, scarlet buoys bobbing and bowing, and ships from the Seven Seas, dwarfed by the river's immensity, crawling up to port. Then there are the storm-swept days when the clouds hang low and the Laurentians send their violet shadows to dance under the green ridges of the waves until the play of color on the water grips your heart with its ethereal and transient beauty. Or, again, there are the sunsets when the river

14

Tugs take charge of a freighter
near Montreal.

15

lies like a tranquil pool of gold; or moon-flooded nights when the water shimmers like beaten silver and ebony hills stand like sentinels under a sparkling heaven.

.   .   .   .

These delights are to come, for we are embarking on a white ship at a point not far from where Cartier's little mediæval vessel landed four centuries ago. The ship noses her way out and turns toward pretty St. Helen's Island (l' Isle Ste. Hélène) which was named more than three hundred years ago for Hélène Boulle, the young bride of Samuel de Champlain. This was for many years the headquarters of the British garrison, in old colonial days, and there are still regimental buildings to be seen there. For generations it has been a favorite picnicking place with Montrealers and now, for the first time, it is connected with the main shores by the great new bridge under which we sail.

East of St. Helen's is a low lying island where, on the night before the surrender of Montreal to General Amherst, in 1760, were burned all the French flags, the white and golden *fleur de lys* of the Bourbon kings which had flown over New France for a hundred and fifty years.

The first town on the southern shore is Longueuil the site of the most picturesque seigneury of the French

17

régime. Charles Le Moyne was the son of an inn-keeper of Dieppe who, from the crews of returning vessels, sitting about the round oak tables of his father's tap-room, astonishing their stay-at-home friends with tales of their adventures, heard fabulous tales of the new colony. In 1654 he came to Canada. He spent four years among the Hurons learning their language, their traits and customs. Later he was granted a seigneury at Longueuil on which, thanks partly to his Canadian bride, young Catherine Primot, who came from Montreal, he prospered vastly. Eventually he was granted letters from the King making him one of the Canadian noblesse. They had fourteen children, seven of them famous sons. The eldest, another Charles Le Moyne, became one of the wealthiest men in New France and, in 1700, was created Baron de Longueuil This is the only French-Canadian title to survive under the British régime, Queen Victoria having confirmed the authenticity of the barony. The present Baron Longueuil lives in England and bears the Scottish name of Grant. At the time of the Conquest of Canada the title had descended to a little girl who grew up to marry, in 1781, Captain David Alexander Grant.

The manor house at Longueuil was the nearest approach to a French château in the new world. It

The old and the new. One of
the white ships passes two
"pin flats" at anchor.

was a great walled dwelling place, with fortified towers, store houses and a chapel, in addition to the dwelling of the Le Moyne family. Nothing remains of the old manor now but the graceful parish church, built on the site and of its old grey stones, and of which one may see the spire among the tree tops.

Among the celebrated brothers of the first Baron Le Moyne were Pierre Le Moyne d'Iberville and Jean Le Moyne de Bienville, the founders of Louisiana and its Governors for a period of nearly forty years. D'Iberville was one of the distinguished sea captains of the eighteenth century, having sailed and fought from the Spanish Main to Hudson Bay with honor and distinction.

Presently we come to Verchères, also on the southern shore, where there is an old tower near the water, and a huge bronze figure of a girl awkwardly carrying a rifle, as a school girl would. This is Madeleine de Verchères, whose story has thrilled every Canadian school child since, in 1692, with two young brothers and an old man of eighty for garrison, she defended the fort of Verchères against an Indian war party.

Next comes Varennes with its twin-spired church, and its old manor house, still standing. This was once

21

the scene of an Iroquois massacre, though one would never guess it from its gentle serenity now.

The town of Sorel stands at the mouth of the Richelieu river, the great highway of the Iroquois from New York state. Down this broad and beautiful stream the bloodthirsty red men travelled again and again to ravage New France until the officers and men of the Carignan-Salières regiment came here to settle in its fertile meadow-lands and so form a living bulwark against the savages. Monsieur Pierre de Sorel, one of these officers, obtained the Seigneury at the mouth of the Richelieu where once before he had been sent to build a fort. This great French regiment, came to New France in 1665, when the colony was shivering in fear of extinction. Its commander, the Marquis de Tracy, was attended by pages in royal livery and valets and grooms to wait upon him. His coming changed New France from a mission station into a brilliant little court, and, for the time at least, he brought security and gave heart to the colonists. Hundreds of the men of his regiment stayed in New France, and it was to supply them with wives—gently born desmoiselles for the officers and stout, hard-working girls for the men—that King Louis sent out his Bride-Ships and more than a thousand brides within ten years time.

A French-Canadian "Pin-flat" or river
barge unloading cordwood, at the old
east-end wharves, Montreal.

23

At Sorel the river begins to broaden into Lake St. Peter, and where it narrows again into the river stream stands Three Rivers, our next port of call.

Three Rivers gets its name from the triple mouth of the St. Maurice, that great river that leads back into the Laurentians and down which have flowed millions of logs to the pulp and paper mills. Up beyond Three Rivers the picturesque life of the shanty men and river men has added a colourful page to industrial life in Canada. It is one of the oldest cities in America, and here are an ancient Ursuline convent and a quaint Anglican church.

On each side of the St. Lawrence, as we sail on, we pass small picturesque French villages with low, white-washed cottages and slender church spires. Side by side lie the old seigneury lands, rich in tradition, and legend, neighbors, though many miles of travel separated manor house from manor house, because of the fact that each faced upon the same highway, the St. Lawrence.

When lands were first granted to settlers in New France, they faced upon the river and ran far back inland, because the river was a necessity to communication and safety. Later, when fathers divided their lands among their sons, they also began at the river, and divided it inland to the farther end. Thus, little by little, these lands came to be mere ribbons, the white cottages popping up side by side, so that to-day the highways of Quebec have that cosy, neighborly air that makes the province unlike any other corner of America.

If you are up very early, before reaching Quebec, you can see in the dawn light the gigantic span of the Quebec Bridge under which the ship passes. Ten years of engineering effort went into its construction, and to-day it stands, a great sweep of steel, linking the north and south shores.

The day is still young when the ship reaches Quebec Basin. Here, on a high bluff stands a great convent and a church with a graceful spire. This is Sillery, one of the first mission posts in Canada, founded and named for a rich knight who sought to win his way into heaven by charity. Here, because they were unable to keep the spotless purity of the habit they had donned in the peaceful seclusion of a Gothic convent in far away France, nursing nuns in early days had to dye their white habits with the stain boiled from bark.

Half hidden in the trees beyond Sillery is Spencer-wood, Quebec's official residence of the King's deputy, the Provincial Lieutenant-Governor. Here hospitality is a tradition, and many times has the great house been

26

"The manor house at Longueuil was
the nearest approach to a French
chateau in the new world."

presided over by sons of French Canada to whom the King had entrusted his royal duties.

Spencerwood was bought originally for the Earl of Elgin, the Governor-General, son of that celebrated Elgin who brought the Greek marbles, since known as the Elgin Marbles, from Athens to the British Museum in London.

And now, looming over the narrowing river, beyond the great Basin, with conscious dignity as the old fortress-capital of New France, stands Quebec.

II

QUEBEC

IF YOU have known Quebec only from her streets and terraces, if you have not viewed her from the river level, with the silver St. Lawrence worshipping at her feet and the purple Laurentians standing like an imperial guard beyond her, you have not seen her in her most romantic mood. From the river, Quebec is a personality—a city of proud and picturesque memories, a silhouette against the sky of towers and turrets, of stately rooftrees, of grey bastions and buttressed walls, of spires and hooded bells. There, in the Citadel that crowns the historic cliffs, the deputy of the King-Emperor holds court to-day just as did the deputy of Henry of Navarre, that hearty Prince of Bearn who was carried to the throne of France on the points of Huguenot swords so long ago. But in Henry's day and in the days of the Kings of France who followed him, the viceroys sometimes had strange guests, naked, copper-skinned savages, with faces, arms and breasts daubed

Three Hundred years ago Huguenot
traders dropped anchor under the
cliffs of Quebec.

31

with red and yellow paint, with feathers in their black hair and human scalps hanging at their belts.

There, upon the bluff, the monastery bells ring at dawn and dusk as they have rung for three hundred years, and within the same convent walls cloistered women teach the little children and nurse the sick as they did when the Thirteenth Louis held court at the Louvre.

A curious city,—a city that has known much of conflict, between red man and white, between church and state, between French and English, between old ideas and new, and yet goes serenely on its way, merging yesterday with to-day and to-morrow.

When Rupert Brooke came to Quebec, his sensitive poet-soul felt and saw its charm and dignity. "Is there any city in the world," he asks, "that stands so nobly as Quebec? It has the individuality and the pride of a city where great things have happened and over which many years have passed."

We sail from the quays of Quebec, as Rupert Brooke did, in one of the white ships of the river fleet; we embark from shores that have known the flavor of adventure ever since Jacques Cartier, the bluff Saint Malo mariner, first set foot upon the sandy beach to confer in sign language with the great Indian sachem, Donnacona, "The King of Canada", whose capital, Stadacona, preceded the white man's city here. Since then these narrow shores under the cliff have felt the tread of thousands of famous feet, sped along their way by high and adventurous hearts. They were lured by the unknown, whether with the hope of finding Marco Polo's Chinese cities, of winning savage souls for the Church, or of trading gewgaws for furs to deck the gallants and adorn the beauties of the courts of Europe.

Here, in the port of Quebec, the great ships of rich Huguenot merchants have come to trade; here, deep in salty hulls, wretched galley slaves have peered longingly at the freedom of the wilderness denied them; and here haughty ships of the line, their sides bristling with guns and with defiant pennants streaming in the air, have cast anchor. This is, by all odds, the most romantic harbour in North America.

Even the veriest novice of a traveller feels the delightful emotion of adventure as the mooring ropes are cast off and the ship noses her way slowly, confidently, out of her place at the quay and comes to grip with the currents of the river. The city recedes slowly and in the uneasy harbour waters the ships dance and twist in fantastic reflections. The early morning sun reaches long golden fingers to polish the window glasses till they

Windmill near Vercheres.

35

glisten like sparks of fire. The battlemented city comes into focus as one great picture, and as we move farther and farther down stream we see the ancient Capital piled up into a silhouetted horizon that is one of the best known, certainly one of the best loved, on the Continent.

Quebec is the only walled city in America. Perhaps her walls were the last to be built as a city's defences. Three nations fought for possession of the city, the French to defend it, the British to seize it, the Americans to force it into the Revolution. Seige upon seige has been laid down upon it, intrigue upon intrigue played upon its fate. Youth has spilled its rich blood in attack and defence, age has dreamed and schemed to hold or take it. It has been loved, envied, hated, feared, and adored.

Out upon the river one realizes the narrowing of the St. Lawrence at this point, the geographical feature which gave Quebec its Indian name. Thanks to the good sense of the French pioneers the beautiful name was never changed to Paris or Amiens or Dieppe as it might so easily have been. Across the river, Levis crouches on its bluffs, with a few shapely spires and bell-turrets breaking the sky line; but Levis has little to offer in interest or beauty to compare with its lovely elder sister, Quebec. But it was there that the British army encamped in the summer of 1759 and bombarded Quebec while the young James Wolfe planned the conquest of the French fortress. The English conquerors of Quebec have been young men, for a hundred and thirty years before young Wolfe made his conquest, the brothers Kirke, of whom we shall hear more at Tadoussac, all under thirty years of age, took Quebec with a gay gallantry that makes the episode a rather pretty tale.

At the turn of the river, on the Levis side, are the shipyards at Lauzon. Quebec has long been famous for its ships, for on both sides of the river trim wooden vessels, famous alike for speed and beauty, were built and launched and sailed by native seamen. And to-day, upon the cliff at Levis, in a yellow brick villa, with a verandah like a ship's bridge, there lives a celebrated old sea dog of sailing ship days, Captain Joseph Bernier, who for sixty years and more has tramped the decks as ship's commander. As a small child in his father's ship he went out to the Crimean war. When the sailing ship days were done he turned north and spent twenty years sailing back and forth between Quebec and the Islands of the far away Arctic, maintaining Canada's rights to the lands bequeathed her by a long race of British explorers.   38

Dredges work tirelessly improving
the ship channel of the St. Lawrence.

The ship from Quebec takes the southern channel around the Island of Orleans, turning away from the lovely Beauport shore where the Montmerency gleams in a silver white cataract and where the old feudal villages of Canada still cluster around their parish churches. But in the southern channel we pass three of the parishes on the quaint little Island of Orléans named by Champlain for a Prince of the royal house of France.

III

ISLE D'ORLÉANS

O RLEANS is a lovable Island. The St. Lawrence seems to have stood guard about its charms, and even to-day it is very little changed. A ferry boat shuttles back and forth between Quebec and the westerly tip of the island, and on its decks you find motor cars jostled by old farm wagons piled high with vegetables and fruits, or perhaps a calf or two on wobbly legs, or pink and white pigs in a crate. Perhaps, too, here and there, will be a box of that celebrated fromage raffiné which has both a history and a bouquet all its own.

There is a drive of about forty miles around the Island,—forty miles of delightful country, of lovely woods, of quaint and undisturbed villages. No matter what the season of the year, the Island has its charm. Nowhere else, I am sure, do violets grow so profusely, or on such long and delicate stems, as they do in its sweet, damp hollows in the May woods. Nowhere is there drowsier content in hot July days when bees hum a summer litany. In the autumn, when the *habitants*

42

The Laurentians as seen from
the Isle of Orleans.

gather in their harvests, as their forefathers have done for a dozen generations, the trees turn to the colors of old wines. Even in mid-winter, when the Island is covered with snow and little pine trees are cut and set as "balises" or "buoys" to mark the highways, even then it has a charm all its own. The only way one can travel there at that time is over the ice bridge in a little red sleigh with a shaggy brown horse to draw you and bear skins up to your chin for warmth. Your driver stands all the way, and now and again he turns to smile good naturedly at you for your whim to cross to the sleeping winter Island.

Ste. Petronille, the youngest parish of the six, though its history is the longest, is the first village at the western tip of the Island. To-day it is chiefly a summer resort for Quebec families, with many comfortable holiday homes. On the north side is the old manor house of the family of Gourdeau de Beaulieu, where there has been a Madame Gourdeau de Beaulieu ever since the days of Eleanor de Grandmaison, a celebrated pioneer whose name stands among those of the first colonists on the Louis Hébert memorial in Quebec.

Less than a stone's throw away is the home of Horatio Walker, the Canadian artist who for nearly half a

45

century, has been painting the *habitants* of the Island, pictures that hang in some of the great collections.

Orleans is an extravagantly fertile little Island. Four hundred years ago Jacques Cartier called it Isle of Bacchus, because of the grape vines that covered it, but it has long since lost its bacchanalian air and settled down to agricultural sobriety.

The next village is St. Laurent. It is here in the channel that the British fleet, in the year of the Conquest, first dropped anchor, and it was at St. Laurent that the English soldiers first set foot on the land they were to camp upon and conquer. The people of the village had fled at the approach of the enemy fleet but the curé pinned a note to the church door addressed to the English commander, imploring him not to demolish the church or burn the village, adding naively: "I would have hoped that you might have arrived earlier so that you could have tasted the vegetables, such as asparagus, radishes, etc., that grow in my garden, and which have now all gone to seed." General James Wolfe granted the old man's request and the church went unmolested.

At the next village, St. Jean, is a celebrated manor house which was recently purchased by a descendant of the original Seigneur, Judge Puliot, who has restored it and furnished it with old Canadian furniture and

46

"We pass small picturesque French
villages with slender church spires."

4

stored its generous attic and basement with relics of the French regime, all of which he gladly shows to those who love old things.

At the eastern end of the Island is the parish of St. François. Here there is a very beautiful old church, built two centuries ago.

On the Island the old handicrafts still flourish. Here, in almost any one of the great, friendly kitchens, one may find Madame and her daughters and daughters-in-law carding or spinning wool, knitting or cutting rags for catalogne, or you may hear from above stairs the musical click-clack of the loom. Here the women of the island still sing their spinning and weaving songs, to lend rhythm to their work. In fact, a young mother, who once responded smilingly to my suggestion that she go on with her flax-spinning while I sat in her kitchen, made the attempt and then stopped her wheel, laughing apologetically because, she said, she could not spin without singing. So with very little urging she sang, too, a gentle wandering song that lent speed and deftness to her fingers, and had a rare sweet air about it, to the accompaniment of the whirring wheel.

On the south shore, too, are still more villages, each with its gentle tenor of life. Each village revolves about its parish church, for each and every one submits to the judgment of the priest who is a veritable father to his flock. Times are changing, though, for the motor car and the radio have made a greater conquest of *habitant* life than a hundred and seventy-five years of British administration. The use of the English language has become more general throughout the Province and now English radio programs penetrate the secluded rural places which are unknown to the tourist.

The story of the sixty thousand French in the Valley of the St. Lawrence, who in less than two centuries, and under alien English rule, have grown into nearly four millions, tenaciously holding to their tongue, their customs, their traditions, in Quebec and in the New England states to which they overflowed, is an epic of the race that rooted itself so firmly in the soil of New France. The story of French Canada is unique. How they came, and settled, and flourished has been told many times.

. . . .

When we leave the Island of Orleans we turn again toward the north shore and pass on our right a group of islands which includes Grosse Isle, the quarantine station. On Grosse Isle is a monument that commemorates a sad story of immigration. This island was bought by the government in 1832 to cope with the

"Between the sloping banks and
ribbon-like farm lands."

scourge of Asiatic cholera, ship's fever and typhus that came to Canada with the tide of home-seekers.

Curiously enough this episode had its origin in the history of the potato. Only a few decades before the Island was bought a scientist was making desperate efforts to have potatoes adopted as a food in France. But no one took him seriously. In Scotland, indeed, the new fangled potato was regarded as the original fruit which caused all the trouble in the Garden of Eden and was denounced as such. Marie Antoinette looked at the growing potatoes and liked their white and golden blossoms so much that she wore them in her hair, for she could imagine no other use for them. But eventually potatoes were recognized as food and when they were introduced into Ireland they flourished beyond belief. To distressed Ireland the potato crops brought peace and plenty. In prosperity the Irish grew and multiplied exceedingly. And then, suddenly, the potatoes failed them. Crop after crop was ruined. Ireland was stricken. There was nothing for the starving people to do but to get out of the wretched land. The undernourished emigrants were crowded into foul-smelling little ships and sent westward to the United States and Canada. They became, of course, prey to disease, and from that time on for two or three decades,

Canada struggled with the awful problem not only of disease, but of the orphaned and destitute emigrants who crowded her towns and cities, helpless, depressed and penniless. Plagues ran through the country like wildfire, and it was in desperation that the quarantine station was opened at Grosse Isle, and any ship that dared to pass it without examination might receive a cannon ball across its bows. In one year alone seven thousand Irish victims of typhus were buried in one titanic grave on Grosse Isle. The memorial recalls these unfortunates and every year the Irish of Quebec make a pilgrimage to the Island in memory of their fellow countrymen.

Salt water reaches up among these islands, although we are still more than four hundred miles from the open sea. Glancing back along the northern channel one can see the gleaming giant towers of the new church of St. Anne that has taken the place of the humble shrine to which the early French sailors of Canada first turned for protection and succor. The Mother of Mary here performs many miracles and enormous pilgrimages are made to her shrine.

East of St. Anne lies the tiny village of St. Joachim, and looming high above the river, dominating, frown-

A passing sail between
Bellechasse and Quebec.

55

ing, is Cap Tourmente, or Cape Storm, eighteen hundred and fifty feet of Laurentian granite.

Here, in the shelter of the cliff, nestling on one of its slopes, is the seminary farm of Laval University. It was Bishop Laval himself who secured this land and established a retreat for those needing rest and seclusion in the course of their studies. It was but a farm which was to supply the seminary at Quebec with grain and cattle, but it is celebrated now because it became the site, in 1685, of the first school of arts and handicrafts in America.

To this farm at Cap Tourmente, Laval brought artists, sculptors, woodcarvers, iron workers, locksmiths and men of many other callings. He brought them from the provinces of France where they were still working in the traditions of the Renaissance and the great days of Francis the First, for the modern school of artists in Paris scorned the outpost society of New France. So when the boys who showed more aptitude for the arts and crafts than they did for theology were sent down to Cap Tourmente to be trained, they learned the methods and technique of an older and finer age. From the hands of these students have come the lovely old houses, the churches with their graceful eaves and slender spires, the ancient altar pieces, the

57

exquisite wood-carvings that have so far escaped the hands of irreverent restorers who sought to "improve" the places of worship in the days of bricks and railways.

The traditions of this old school, handed down from generation to generation in the same families of architects and artists, have persisted to this day, slender though the links have grown. But yonder in St. Joachim, until the year 1928, lived old Louis Jobin, with the gentle face and flowing beard of a biblical saint, who still carved Christ upon the Crucifix, Virgins, and St. Annes, and serene St. Josephs for the parish churches. We shall hear more of Louis Jobin and his wood carving when we reach Cape Trinity.

The waters hereabouts have always been difficult to navigate. Many are the stories told of the adventures encountered here by seamen before the days of charts and navigation signals. Even to-day it requires care and skill.

The St. Lawrence since the days of Champlain has bred hardy pilots. They began with a Scotsman, Abraham Martin, who came out with Champlain and was named King's Pilot. His father had been involved in schemes to get Mary Queen of Scots secretly out of England and out of the way of Queen Elizabeth. When his schemes failed he had to flee to France and

A cargo of lumber bound up
to Quebec from the lower gulf.

thus it was that his son came to be in the service of the French on the St. Lawrence.

During the French régime the river was never properly surveyed and the pilots conspired to keep its navigation as much of a mystery as possible. When, in 1759, Quebec heard that a British fleet was in the river on its way to Quebec, its defenders considered sinking a few ships here in La Traverse to stop their progress. But so sure were they that the Englishmen could not negotiate the dangers of rocks and reefs that they eventually left La Traverse to attend to itself. Meanwhile Admiral Saunders had captured several French pilots and forced them into service. One of these was a hot-headed little man who boldly told the British what he thought of them. He warned them that presently most of their scalps would be hanging on the ramparts at Quebec and that few, if any, of their ships would ever get home again. He happened to be put aboard the *Goodwill* whose master, a certain "Old Killick", was just as hot-headed as the pilot.

The British fleet had used Louisburg as a rendezvous and when it sailed up the Gulf and river, some eighty ships in all, it was forced to travel slowly and take soundings as it went. The celebrated Captain Cook, who later was to circumnavigate the world, was one of the officers in charge of soundings.

Presently, the *Centurion*, a warship of fifty guns, dropped anchor in La Traverse, the first of the fleet to get so far, and not long afterwards along came the *Goodwill* with its proud old captain and its audacious pilot.

There had been more than one occasion on which "Old Killick" would have enjoyed throwing the little pilot over board but Admiral Saunders had issued strict orders that the pilots were to be tolerated, no matter what happened. But though he might be tolerated, "Old Killick" had decided he need not be respected. When they got to La Traverse he chased the pilot from the bridge and declared that he would take the *Goodwill* through La Traverse himself. The Frenchman stormed and declared that they would all be lost. "Perhaps so," fired back the old captain, "but, dam'me, I'll show you that an Englishman shall go where a Frenchman dare not show his nose." So, standing as far forward over the water as he could, and judging by color and ripples on the surface, the captain zig-zagged his ship through the dangerous passage without touching a rock or a sandbar, as neatly as the best of pilots could have done it. The French pilot watched him with consternation, demanding if he had not been through before. When he was assured that "Old Killick" had never in all his life seen La Traverse he threw up his hands to Heaven as at something beyond his comprehension.

IV

THE LAURENTIANS

CAP TOURMENTE is the first of the great imposing capes that reach down so majestically to the river, for the Laurentians have been gradually encroaching upon the St. Lawrence and henceforth they march with us all the way down the picturesque north shore. These are the oldest mountains in the world, mere roots of the stupendous range, higher, so say the geologists, than the Rockies, which towered over eastern America in that primeval day that is hidden in the mists of legendary lore. The ice age ground down the mountains and crushed and polished the grey granite of the Laurentians to the rolling, friendly hills that we see to-day. Nestling high in these glorious hills one may find sandy beaches and sea shells that speak eloquently of eons of years ago when the sea lashed itself over the mountains of to-day. Morris Longstreth writes affectionately of these mountains, "old and magnanimous and worn with the weathers of all time".

"They satisfy the soul's longing for breadth and height and they offer her the inimitable beauty of antiquity . . ." he writes, "They are full of contours that surprise and secret places refreshed with little streams. . . . They offer a prospect familiar and comprehensible and yet so vast as never to be wholly comprehended, making one's heart grateful to them past forgetting."

Indeed they are full of surprises. Every mile onward gives a new contour, a new vista, a new delight. The valleys beyond are indescribably beautiful, with fields wrung acre by acre from the forest by patient and simple hands, patterned with split rail fences and studded with stone piles added to generation by generation. Here and there villages cuddle into the shoulder of a hill, or nestle in a fold in the valley.

It is awesome to think of the unnumbered hills that stand regimented northward, over the vast territories of northern Quebec. Even from the river we can see them crowding together, fold after fold, receding away into the distance, fading into glamorous tints that hint at far away and mysterious places. To-day's men and women, almost pitifully dependent upon the fabric of life they have woven with such pride, look into these eternal hills with awe, for it takes a big soul,—bigger than this tense and speedy civilization generally breeds,

—to go into these mighty places alone and without fear. We look back upon the Indians and their myths and legends, their gods and their superstitions, with pity or amusement, forgetting that these red men and women lived among these hills, fed and clothed themselves, lived, moved and had their being, under conditions which would make of the average white man to-day a shivering, starving, helpless madman in a few weeks time.

When we want to get back beyond the reach of civilization, even the simple civilization of the *habitant,* into the solitudes of the hills, into the places from which life itself seems to come, we are still dependent upon the remnant of the Indian race for guidance; and in the souls of these Laurentian guides there still lingers something of the pagan simplicity that comes from living close to the sources of life.

.   .   .   .

Presently we shall come to Baie St. Paul which lies along the mouth of the Riviére du Gouffre, in one of the most beautiful valleys in eastern Canada. From the river there is a glimpse of low fertile lands running far back into the purple hills, with the slopes below the thick forest ridges retrieved and set to the service of the plough. Here the low white houses and the silvery-

66

Ships from the Seven Seas move
up and down the river.

grey barns speak of a people devoted to the soil. This was the first French settlement upon which the ships from France came on their passage up to Quebec, for early in the history of the colony some hardy souls saw the richness of the valley.

This is one of the settlements where old types of craft still survive. Here every steep roofed cottage has its spinning wheel and its loom. On the hillsides roam the sheep that clothe the farmers and their families, provide the blankets and the coverlets for their beds and the hangings for their windows. There in the fields grows the flax from which Madame makes the coarse, soft linens for her home.

The river is twenty miles wide here, and some miles off shore is Isle aux Coudres, one of the most interesting spots in the St. Lawrence, but difficult of access. It was named long ago by Jacques Cartier, and it was settled early in the eighteenth century by families, whose descendants are still living there, spinning, weaving, singing their old songs, dancing their old dances to the tunes which the fiddler learned from his father, telling their long and amusing tales, (for the *raconteur* is a village big-wig) with all the naturalness of the Norman adventurers in the days of the Great Louis.

The river between the Island and the North Shore

69

has long been a shelter for ships. Under the French kings all ships used the north channel and only of more recent years have the big ships sailed away to the south instead. This was also a rendezvous for the British fleet under Admiral Saunders in 1759, his scout ships having dropped anchor here to await the arrival of the main fleet. So great and so picturesque was this armada of ships of the line, frigates, transports, and supply ships, that when the first of them had reached Isle aux Coudres, the last of them was still at Cacouna, opposite Tadoussac, nearly fifty miles away. What a sight it must have been, with the great river studded with these eighteenth century ships, with black guns staring from their oaken hulls, their sea-stained sails curved against the winds and flags and pennants flying!

Along the shores the French, in consternation, set fire to their beacons, from point to point, all the way up stream to warn Quebec that her beseigers were on the way. These beacon fires were the only means of long distance communication in those days and the colonists very cleverly developed such a code that in the long winters they were able to talk from one settlement to another across ice-bound rivers by their bon-fires, and thus exchange the news.

·   ·   ·   ·

The old style French sailing barge
is a fast disappearing type of craft
on the St. Lawrence.

They are astonishingly alike, the homes you see along the way, when once you find your way indoors. The kitchen is the living-room where the one big three-decker stove serves as furnace and cooking stove. The parlor is a place of washed and shining aloofness, reserved within drawn blinds for ceremonial visits, for weddings and funerals, with sacred pictures, portraits of brothers in the priesthood and sisters who have taken the veil. Perhaps there is a coffin plate or two surrounded with funeral rosettes, framed upon the walls. Or, under a well polished glass dome, may be a "petit Jésus" in delicately embroidered clothes, its wax head covered with hair from some little golden head that has already grown up to be old and wise. But in the kitchen all is pleasant comfort. Grandpère, with a creased and wrinkled brown face, pulls at his short pipe, stuffed with "tabac Canadien," and rocks the youngest grandchild on his knee. The next little lad, so recently dispossessed of the place on grandpère's knee, rocks himself in a diminutive chair nearby.

They are spotless, as a rule, these homes ruled over by the convent-trained women of Quebec. Each one in the family, which is likely to be large, with brothers and sisters, as well as grandparents to share the tasks and pleasures of the farm, has his rocking-chair, and

73

they rock endlessly, rythmically, each one in his own time and speed. Indeed there may be rockers long enough for four, made, they tell you, smiling broadly, for a pair of lovers, and a pair of chaperons, sitting one at each end to keep a sleepy watch upon the courtship.

The Baie St. Paul district has been rich in inspiration to Canadian artists. Clarence Gagnon, a French Canadian, and one of the most advanced of the Quebec group, paints of the homely, colorful things of Quebec village life with both tenderness and skill. He has won distinction on two continents and has immortalized some Quebec hamlets in the process.

Paul Caron, whose river scenes help to illustrate this volume, has found a wealth of material in the valley of the lower St. Lawrence. Mr. Caron is popularly known for his vivid depiction of *habitant* life. In woodcuts, water-colors and oils he has portrayed the colorful yet simple existence in rural Quebec.

Two members of the Group of Seven, who have done so much to create a distinct national school of art in Canada, have painted in this district. Arthur Lismer says that "Art is a way of life. It is not entertainment nor professionalism. It is a necessity." Writing of him in *A Canadian Art Movement, The Story of the Group of Seven,* F. B. Housser says: "There is no domain from

74

which he would banish it. Down on Isle aux Coudres and Isle d'Orleans he found habitant women making hooked mats, homespuns and catalognes, not as articles of service but for the fun of doing them. The women stow their mats and catalognes away in cupboards by hundreds without using them. Lismer claims they are creations of necessity and that the making of them helps these women to live contentedly without sinking down beneath the weight of drudgery as so many women do on the prairies who have no creative outlet." Mr. Lismer has sketched and painted these people in their own haunts.

A. Y. Jackson, another member of the group, was born in Montreal and had an early instinctive knowledge of Quebec and its people. After three and a half years service at the front in the Great War he went to Quebec to paint, "lured by the seclusion and quiet of French Canada after the wrack of war".

"He is always at home in his Georgian Bay and Quebec canvases," writes Mr. Housser. "The rugged poetry of the two districts is in harmony, though in outer fact they so widely differ.

"No one ever described French-Canadian Quebec so well as Adjutor Rivard in his book, *Chez Nous* which Jackson has illustrated. Rivard makes the boy ask

'What do you think of it, Uncle Jean? People keep talking of country. Speakers have the words forever on their lips and writers on the tips of their pens. What *is* one's country, Uncle Jean?'

" 'Two or three times he drew at his pipe in silence and blew a cloud of smoke; then with eyes still bent on the distant woods, a wide sweep of his hand embraced the fields, meadows and forests; and thus he spoke:

" 'Our country—it is that. Over there to the sou'-west lives François le Terrien, and beyond him Pierre the son of Dennis and then other neighbors and other neighbors again. To the nor' west we have the big Guillaume and old Ambrose's two sons; and more neighbors and yet more neighbors to the end of the concession and the end of the Parish. Now let us say—I do not know precisely whether it is the case but it ought to be, let us say that every man of them like myself is on land that belonged to his people. You would have a whole parish rooted in the soil, wouldn't you? And then in the centre stands the church, alongside it the burying ground; close by the curé's house and the curé himself inside it. After our parish there is another parish and another and another, all alike and each with its church steeple, its curé and its buried dead, its old soil worked by fathers and fathers' fathers which one loves more

76

than oneself. There you have it, this country of ours!'

"This feeling of habitant Quebec which Adjutor Rivard has given us in *Chez Nous* Jackson gives us in paint. He has hundreds of sketches gathered between Levis and Baie St. Paul. He loves to find a winter road where the snow tracks play hide and seek around the drifts. . . . There are the blue hills you see across the river in so many of his pictures. Jackson likes to paint them in the early spring when the snow is patchy on the steeps. These pictures make one love the French-Canadian people. They depict old and settled communities of home-loving folk where the strain of life is eased by simple faith."

Canadian artists of the new school are men as much at home in the hidden villages and in the solitudes, as in their own studios. Summer and winter you will find them with pack-sacks, canoes or snowshoes, wandering over the hinterlands, camping out on rocky shores, cooking over their own camp fires, sleeping under the stars, as hardy as voyageurs.

The sail from Baie St. Paul to Murray Bay is one of increasing impressiveness. Here the Laurentians seem to crowd down to the river's edge and the tiny red and white lighthouses look like toys tucked away on ledges in the cliffs. Headland after headland starts out from the coast as if set upon a stage by some artist drunk with power.

At the east end of Isle aux Coudres is the cliff of Les Eboulements, which got its name from the landslides which changed so much of the shore here in the terrible year of 1663, when as one old chronicle says, "the river ran white from Quebec to Tadoussac for three months." From early spring to autumn the tremors persisted daily until even the white whales "made piteous noises". It was a dark day everywhere in colonial affairs and the torments of nature seemed the final word in misery. There is a village here, too, at Les Eboulements.

The next village set down between the hills is Ste. Irenée, which is also a popular summer resort.

Every dip in these hills gives access to fresh wonders beyond, where there are frothy streams and firm pink trout. Here you will see men leaning on the ship's rail with the light of longing in their eyes while they think of star-hung nights under the pine trees, of crackling logs upon a camp fire, of flies that sing their way onto the streams, and of fish that nibble.

In these hills men seize for a little moment something of the old freedom of the race, for out there telephones and stock brokers have no part in the scheme of exis-

78

"The Manoir Richelieu resting in
its baronial beauty on the ledge
overlooking the river."

tence. Nothing matters but the hour, the fish, the trail. The ticker ticks in vain when bait is the most vital subject under the heavens and a motor-car, in perspective, seems the clumsiest vehicle ever conceived by man, when the slim canoe responds to every blade stroke as though it was a caress.

.   .   .   .

Presently we sail on toward a picturesque headland at Pointe au Pic, which tapers down to a bluff above the river. Nestling on its shoulder, over the water, is a great baronial château that seems to have grown up with New France, to embody all the rich traditions of old feudal days, an intimate part of the north shore which has been so long the stage of a dramatic colonial history. But the great grey stone château has no tradition of knightly wars or feudal ambitions behind it. It is a very modern business miracle.

On this site for many, many years stood the old, rustic Manoir Richelieu. In the autumn of 1928 it was destroyed by fire, its dry old timbers making a titanic bonfire. Within a few days the Canada Steamship Lines had decided to rebuild. The task was a colossal one. Winter was approaching. Murray Bay was a hundred miles from the nearest base of supplies. But the attempt was made. Within a year the Manoir was

79

rebuilt, all the work being carried on under a wooden shell which kept off the frost, and on the usual opening day of the summer season in the following year, the most beautiful hotel in Canada was ready for the inflocking summer visitors.

Some day historians will see in this vigorous and enterprising age something of the romance which we now reserve for times of long ago. They will see in the conception and achievement of tasks of this sort something of the same spirit that in less prosaic days drove men far afield for adventure and conquest.

The new Manoir was to be an expression of the French régime, not of manorial life which was simple enough in colonial days, even at its best, but an expression of the France which ruled, France of the court and salon.

The Manoir which rests so intimately upon the hill side is the result. Its copper roofs are gradually gathering the rich patina that only time can give. Its vines creep slowly toward the eaves; gardens, achieved as if by magic, look as though they had known endless seasons there.

Bridle trails lead into the thick and scented woods, and back beyond reach of the riders are the luring valleys where for a thousand years sunlight has spent

80

itself, color has run riot, and the perfume of balsam and cedar have drenched the lonely hills, with seldom a human soul to share their treasures.

V

MURRAY BAY

MURRAY BAY is one of the oldest summer playgrounds in Canada. In the infancy of the steamship, a century ago, we find that the *Waterloo* called at Pointe au Pic on a pleasure trip. It was a special treat to friends in Quebec and Montreal when they were invited down to visit at one or other of the manor houses on Murray Bay. Before the Confederation of the Dominion so many English families had established themselves there that they founded a Protestant church that still serves the summer colony. After the assassination of Abraham Lincoln it was to Murray Bay that his nerve-wracked widow was sent for the healing air and the peace and serenity that possesses these river outposts of the Laurentians. For later generations the Manoir Richelieu has been the centre of the holiday life at Murray Bay and when, in September, 1928, the friendly old wooden hotel was burned many believed that a great tradition was lost forever. But, June, 1929, found a new and greater Manoir, rich in the spirit of the past, lifting its towers on the site of the old hotel.

Murray Bay itself is a lovely patch of water lying in a contour of the shore line. It can be a tricky place for ships, as Champlain found when he named it Mal Baie. But often you may find it lying like a great opal, with the lights changing from rose and blue to dusky amethyst on its tranquil face. As the tide recedes great flocks of sea gulls come streaming in on outstretched pinions, dipping, swerving, gliding, with the inimitable grace of these great birds that seem to move as swift as thought and with as little effort. The sand-bar in the Bay is one of their favorite resting places, and on the salty sands they gather in unnumbered companies.

The friendly hills around Murray Bay are threaded with motor roads that lead to the farmlands in the valleys and beyond them into the fishing country, celebrated the world over for its sport as well as for its impressive beauty, its magic starlit nights and its days of exhilaration.

The first farmers came to Murray Bay more than two and a half centuries ago under the feudal schemes of The Great Intendant.

Monsieur Talon was the first and the greatest of Canadian Intendants, and came to Canada in the golden age of the French regime. He was to New France what Colbert was to old France. He built ships and sent them trading with Canadian goods; he founded a brewery that the colonists might drink beer of their own brewing; he searched for coal and iron and copper, encouraged and making of woollen and linen cloths and for the first time taught the Canadians to depend upon themselves instead of trusting to the supplies of a paternal government. He was handsome and genial, and a clever man to boot, and he it was who gave Mal Baie its first Seigneur. This was Phillipe Gauthier, Sieur de Comporte, who came with his settlers to wrestle with the wilderness. But half a century after he came to Mal Baie the King of France bought back the seigneury and added it to the King's Domain; and that is how it was that when New France came under British sway these crown lands were waiting for new masters.

It will be recalled that in the wars between England and France, and after the suppression of Prince Charlie's armies in 1745, that the kilt was forbidden. Under wiser diplomacy the fighting Scots were incorporated into the British army and allowed to wear the kilt as their uniform. The Fraser Highlanders made up one of the regiments raised under that plan, and of it more perhaps is heard than of any other single regiment serv-

84

On the horizon there are always ships.

ing under Wolfe in the seige of Quebec. Many of the
men in that regiment had French sympathies, and many
of its officers spoke French so well that they were used
for deceiving the French-Canadians in several encoun-
ters between British parties and French sentries. For
years there had been a friendship between France and
Scotland, for a Scottish princess had been queen of
France and a French princess queen of Scotland. It
was chiefly from France that Scottish rebellions had
been directed.

So, after the fall of New France, it was the French-
speaking Scots who first made friends with the native
Canadians.

Two officers of the Fraser Highlanders, John Nairn
and Malcolm Fraser, had already learned something
about Mal Baie and they petitioned the Governor, General Murray, for grants of land upon which to establish
themselves and their men.

General Murray divided the old seigneury between
them, and John Nairn received the lands to the west of
the river which was re-named Murray River, and Malcolm Fraser had the lands to the east.

To this day the manor houses built by the two Scots
still stand. The Fraser manor-house, now the home of
the Cabots of Boston, has been considerably augmented

and reconstructed as a result of damage done by an earthquake a few years ago. It is a delightful place with the full flavor of seigneurial days. The Nairn house is almost unchanged. Even its old barns are intact, and although the old Nairn furnishings are no longer there the house is full of important mementoes of the great old Scotsman. There is the old Nairn library, with rare old first editions that came to Murray Bay as they came off the eighteenth and nineteenth century presses, side by side with old favorites that he brought out from his old home when he settled here, books that had belonged to his father and grandfather before him. Here too are rare old documents, accounts books, military journals, and many other things of historical and romantic interest, swords, miniatures, portraits and innumerable relics of a gallant family. The Nairn family died out in the third generation, and their story is told in Professor Wrong's *A Canadian Manor and its Seigneurs*. The seigneury has never been sold, but has passed on by inheritance to its present owners, the Grey family.

At the Manoir Richelieu there are two fine murals painted by C. W. Jefferys, R.C.A., the most celebrated Canadian contemporary historical painter, portraying the coming of Sieur de Comporte in the French regime, and the coming of Nairn and Fraser in the British re-

88

gime. These are two great, brilliant canvases, embodying the very essence of this old Laurentian romance.

There are really three settlements at Murray Bay. There is Pointe-au-Pic, where the ships dock, the village of La Malbaie, sometimes still called Murray Bay, at the head of the bay, and Cap à l'Aigle, to the east. These have a vastly augmented population in the summer time, for families from many parts of the United States and Canada have summer homes here.

This is the home of the famous Murray Bay homespun and Murray Bay blankets and hundreds of little homes hereabouts are employed in weaving to meet the demand of the more sophisticated world for the native products which have been the common things of existence to these people since the first sheep nibbled at the grasses on the hillsides by the Bay.

Learned men and women have made a study of this old industry, and artists have helped to foster the primitive designs and discourage the tendency to fall in with easy modern methods. They have urged the spinners and weavers to continue using their native vegetable dyes and to depend only upon their own ingenuity for patterns for their hooked rugs.

William Carless, of the department of architecture

at McGill, who has written a delightful little booklet on homespun says:

"Under homely, traditional conditions this essentially native industry is pursued. Once the people's sole source of supply for woolen fabrics, Canadian homespun has survived the competition of modern production and is highly appreciated for its artistic appearance and good wearing qualities. . . . We may regret the change which has banished to oblivion the looms that used to be in constant use in every farmhouse, but we have the satisfaction to know that one of the old crafts is still providing employment for thousands. For this we have to thank those people who in the last twenty-five years have done so much in this respect."

How the *habitants* used their homespun we see in the scores of pictures of Canadian life from the brushes of Krieghoff, a German artist, who spent thirteen years in Quebec in the middle of the last century, and whose canvases are prized items of Canadiana to-day.

In Murray Bay you will also find French Canadian cabinet makers busy in their little workshops by the roadside, making fine and beautiful furniture. They have inherited a gift for woodwork and to-day not only do they make native furniture but they can make beautiful copies as well. I have seen all sorts of things,

90

from good copies of really beautiful old Chippendale chairs to pieces in the fashion of the Art Moderne. They are clever artisans, as they have always been, for I have seen pieces, made back in the French regime, in which native cabinetmakers had the magnificent courage to reproduce designs of the finest Louis Fourteenth tradition, and they did it extraordinarily well, in native woods.

For many, many years the Blake family, of Toronto, have spent their summers here. W. H. Blake wrote intimately and delightfully of this country and its people. Since boyhood he was one of the worshippers in the little Protestant church. You find it to-day standing on the street of the French village, a curious and beautiful note in this essentially Norman land, with its beautiful grey stone walls built in the early English fashion. Mr. Blake speaks of this church as "resting upon twin Anglican and Presbyterian pillars, the portals standing open to beliefs widely sundered in theory. The only credo is 'I believe'." This was a little pioneer united church, for all the Protestant denominations share its friendly shelter. It is full of memorials of those who served in or worshipped in it. It has a memorial to those gallant lads who turned their backs upon the pleasant leisure of Murray Bay to go and defend its

peace on the battlefields of France. The French voices
in the little war stricken villages behind the lines must
have made them think of the far away Laurentian
villages.

Behind the church the land slips way to the shore.
This is the God's Acre of the church, but there is only
one grave there. It must be a pleasant resting place,
for it is W. H. Blake, who wrote with poetic tenderness
of the place and its people, who lies there. His grave
is almost shrine-like, with the friendly trees for shelter.
A flat slab of granite bears his name, and a long, slender,
incised cross, cut by the village stone mason, one of his
many friends who did the task in loving gratitude to this
good friend of his race. The inscription is wholly ade-
quate,—"The spirit of man is the candle of God".

In one of his books, called *In A Fishing Country*,
Mr. Blake talks of the country around Murray Bay and
of the New York doctor who, as far back as 1882,
helped to make it famous by prescribing its air as a
tonic to jaded society folk. Unfortunately for most of
the visitors they come here only in July and August,
while Mr. Blake gives June and September as the finest
months in the year. June he loved for its delicate air,
its blossoming trees and flowers and exquisite colors.
September he loved for sparkling jewel-like days, the

extravagant beauty of the maples, mountain ash, Indian pear and wild cherry. He speaks of May as a month of youth and delight, and October for the "new minted gold of the birches, the blueberries' tongues of flame."

Mr. Blake was also the translator of Louis Hémon's classic story of pioneer Quebec, *Maria Chapdelaine*. His version has a poetic quality about it, which makes it probably the finest English translation.

There are two golf links at Murray Bay. One is in the village, near the water's edge, in that curious depression where the glaciers, eons of years ago, deposited sand mounds which have puzzled students of the earth's history ever since. Sometimes archaeologists have burrowed into them thinking to find vestiges of some vanished race, but it seems that they are due to a freak of the titanic ice fields that ground their relentless ways over the continent so long ago.

The other golf course is that laid out for the Manoir Richelieu. It is a thousand feet above the river, built into the contours of the hills, in settings of such imperial beauty that how a golfer can keep his mind upon his game is much more than I can understand. This is one of the finest golf courses in the world. Here the panorama is twice as great as it is at the Manoir below. However, the course does not rest upon the laurels of the scenic excellence, but provides the rarest sport to please a golfer's soul.

The Manoir Richelieu course is spread out on a ledge of the mountainside called "The Ridge". From number one tee, just behind the clubhouse, there is a bird's-eye view of the whole picturesque sweep of it. The three divisions of the course, the Valley, the Forest, and the Park, can be easily seen. The Valley, devoid of trees and dotted with sanded traps and the verdant oases of the putting greens, runs through the center of the course, sloping away from you towards the river. The Forest, with the graceful swaths of the fairways running through it, lies to the left of the Valley. The Park is the undulating, slightly wooded region lying to the right. The first nine holes run chiefly through the Forest, while the incoming nine lie in the Valley and the Park.

Lost in contemplation of the view from the first tee you will understand why it is said that the glory of the scenery is the chief hazard of the golfer at this Canadian resort. One is tempted merely to stand and look! So it is just possible that on your first visit you will be recalled to your morning's engagement with par or bogey by hearing a voice behind you: "M'sieur, votre ball est en tee."

It is your French-Canadian caddy speaking. You face about. The moment has come for your first shot at Murray Bay.

.　　.　　.　　.

Fifty miles back from the shore and two thousand feet above sea level is an isolated lake that has sea fish a thousand miles from home. "The retiring sea," says Mr. Blake, "must have left this rare Arctic charr behind after the departure of the ice . . . to testify as to the line and order of events."

These woods are also full of old French and Indian trails that were made in years long gone by, by the feet of huntsmen and traders and explorers. In the winter months skiiers who come to Murray Bay for winter sports use these old trails to explore the forests. Murray Bay was a familiar spot to these travellers of trail and stream, and within living memory Indians still made canoes here for a living.

Only a day's travel inland on these luring waters of the Murray River the adventurer comes upon a river gorge that rivals in majesty and untamed solitude the very Saguenay itself.

After hobnobbing with villagers and fishermen and adventurers we shall go back to the Manoir Richelieu, resting in its baronial beauty on the ledge overlooking

the river. The Manoir has little of the atmosphere of a
hotel and as much of the air of feudal hospitality as it
is possible to capture in this day. It is considered the
most beautiful hotel in Canada. From its long terraces
there is a landscape of forty or fifty miles upon which
to rest eyes cramped for most of the year between city
walls.

Since the days when Governors-General of Canada
came to Murray Bay aboard wood burning side-wheel
steamers, the Manoir Richelieu has been one of the fea-
tures of the lower St. Lawrence country. With the
representatives of the King came young *aides de camp*
—young men with sweeping cavalry moustaches in the
mid-Victorian manner, with names that were to become
famous in later years as colonial administrators or com-
manders of army corps. And romances were frequent
which carried Canadian brides to the peerage of
England.

Through these years and down to our own times the
Manoir Richelieu has preserved its tradition of graceful
and dignified hospitality. Never have the glaring characteristics so common to the summer and winter resort
entered into the life at Murray Bay.

In the French Manoir style and in the heart of the
grand seigneurial country the Manoir is born of 18th

century France. The furnishings and the very atmosphere of its public rooms disclose a reverence for all that was fine in the life of two hundred years ago. In the bedrooms the beauty of *habitant* handicraft has been preserved by the use of homespun fabrics with all their vigorous colour and design. The whole conception is quite unique in hotels. Certainly never before has an eighteenth century atmosphere been so successfully blended with the luxuries of modern living.

The ballroom of the Manoir is a separate building with a low-sweeping roof and a round tower. Beside the ballroom building is the swimming pool, and at noon, while an orchestra plays and the breeze murmurs in the pines, this is the setting for a picture of vigorous youth swimming and diving while perhaps the less strenuous sun themselves with magnificent idleness.

If you happen to be sleeping in the eastern end of the Manoir you may find that the Murray Bay sunrises will steal right into your room and wake you from the illimitable depths of slumber into which that Laurentian air plunges you.

There was a June morning when the sun called me up shortly after three o'clock so that I had a chance to watch the Master Artist mixing his colors for the painting of a summer day. Over Cap à l'Aigle were banners

97

of rose and gold and blue and under my startled eyes
the rose turned to gold and the gold to cyclamen. The
horizon was like a scarf of colored gauze and through
it color and light and day itself pulsed up from the
inexhaustible East. Far to the south across the river
was a blue ridge, and northwards the faintly purple
headlands "still remembering night". The bowl of the
sky faded slowly to azure as the light swept upward.
Thin clouds grew rosy as wine as the brush strokes of
dawn grew longer and swept around the arc of the sky.
Over everything was a pale golden glamor, as the trees
swayed in the dawn wind like singing worshippers while
the sun was born of the sea.

Here for untold ages the wandering savages saw
the glory of each new day. That was in the days before
we cramped them with our unaccustomed philosophies.
So, there is nothing I can better wish a guest here than
a wakeful dawn as panacea for human ills and vain
ambitions.

There is a pleasant diversion within doors at the
Manoir in reading the story of Canada from the fifteen
hundred and more rare Canadian prints and paintings
which are hung upon its walls. These have been col-
lected for the Manoir and are intended to reconstruct

98

pictorially the life of the past three hundred years in New France and in British North America.

The largest canvas in the collection is one showing Columbus before Isabella of Spain. This was painted by Brozik, in 1884, and hung for some thirty years in the Metropolitan Museum of Art in New York before it was secured, against strong competition, for this collection. In it the middle-aged queen is shown listening tensely to the pale and earnest dreamer who is asking for ships in which to sail westwards in search of the fabulous East. Near her stand her attendants, with her jewel cases, out of which she bought for him the ships in which he found the new world.

The murals by C. W. Jefferys are part of this collection, as are also canvasses by A. Sherriff Scott, including a portrait of Hélène de Champlain and copies of portraits of General Murray and of Cardinal Richelieu after whom the Manoir was named and whose mighty will reached across the seas in the early days of the colony to direct the work of French Imperialism in America.

There are among other things six rare views by Harvey Smyth, twelve by Richard Shortt, twenty-three by Sir Daniel Wilson, others by James Hope, and innumerable men who caught with pen and brush earlier days in Canadian life. There is also a very rare print of Wolfe dating to 1760, the year after the Conquest. However, there is a catalogue to this collection available, which is itself a valuable reference book of Canadiana.

Once you have breathed the air of Murray Bay, compounded of equal parts of breezes from the sea and essence of Laurentian pine, you will not forget this lovely North Shore, nor will you be happy until you return again on a summer day or perhaps in the winter when the log-fires roar up the chimneys of the Manoir and there is skiing and tobogganing on the hills.

We set sail at last from Murray Bay to follow again the massive North Shore towards the Saguenay.

VI

THE PORTALS OF THE SAGUENAY

AT LAST we have come to the great amphitheater on which so much of drama, of romance and of mystery have been played, the meeting place of the waters that flow from the Great Lakes, through the St. Lawrence, and those that flow from the northern watershed beyond Lake St. John by the Saguenay. Waters that started in tiny springs and rainpools thousands of miles part, here rush together on their triumphant march to the sea.

Here at this juncture floated the fleets of the French adventurers facing the twin routes and debating upon the highway of their choice. Up the Saguenay the way leads eventually to the hinterlands, James Bay and Hudson's Bay and the great white Arctic. By the St. Lawrence lay the Great Lakes and the routes across the prairies to the Rockies and the sea beyond. Up each of these the adventurers went eventually, but at the end of each they looked for—China! Mystery lay up the

battlemented Saguenay. The St. Lawrence, mighty as
it was, still seemed the kindlier river with good green
foothold along the way for men perhaps grown weary
of the sea.

Some of the age old mystery of the Saguenay still
remains, and when the ship turns out for that long
wheeling approach, circling treacherous reefs and sand
bars, even the unimaginative must feel something of
the zest for adventure which stirred its old explorers.

This strange body of water is half river and half
fiord. Its navigators, even up to Chicoutimi, seventy
miles away, have to contend with tides. It was formed,
so geologists say, by a titanic wrenching of the earth's
crust that left this great slit in the Laurentians. For
centuries the awe-stricken said that the river had no
floor, that it was impossible to plumb its dark depths
between the over hanging cliffs. This fallacy still per-
sists, though it is truly deep enough to be impressive
without fable to bolster up its claims. Perhaps much
of the sombre tradition in its history is due to the very
human attributes of jealousy and fear. Those in possession said to those who would like to have been in
possession: "This is a savage river. It is the River of
Death. Look at its gloomy walls, look at its dark
and mysterious waters. Stay out." The Indians passed

Pulpwood laden ships are
common sights.

this tradition to the white men, and the trader handed it on to the colonists.

I heard a very shrewd conclusion reached on this subject of the overwhelming effect of the Saguenay upon men and women. It was an artist who spoke, an artist who drew on all the foibles of human nature to feed his philosophy. He wondered in what spirit most men approach the Saguenay and its massive cliffs. Did they come so swollen with self-importance that suddenly, in the face of Nature in this stark and simple form, they realized with a withering insight how small a part of the universe they constituted? If man has a proper estimate of his own place in the scheme of life why should he be suddenly stricken with a palsy of fear when he sees something even so vast and majestic as this strange river?

Perhaps we have at last overcome this legacy of mediaevalism and can see something in the Saguenay besides its gloom, see something of the glory of its color, the rhythm of its hills, the play of light upon its rocks, the nuances of green in its wind-beaten trees.

It is reasonable to imagine that long before our recorded history of the Saguenay white men drifted here in Viking ships. Carved hulls, under square sails, driven by long oars glittering with sea water, doubtless turned in at the mouth of the river. Viking shields hung over the gunwales, painted and studded, and perhaps stained with the blood of conquests, while the Norsemen, driven across from Greenland and Iceland, either by contrary winds or by their lust for adventure, gazed in amazement at this new land. These men of the north perhaps had less fear of the fiord-like stream and they may have sailed and rowed up to see its towering cliffs.

It is easy enough to understand the superstitions and fear of the sixteenth and seventeenth century crews of the explorers' ships. Jacques Cartier was a mediaeval seaman. "Both the first and the last," says Colonel William Wood, "to appear on Canadian inland waters." It was four years afterwards before Fletcher of Rye invented a rig by which a ship could beat to windward with sails trimmed fore and aft, and with his invention began the age of modern seamanship. But in addition to contrary winds Cartier had to sail against the winds of superstition. "Men of that time," goes on Colonel Wood, "were quite ready to mutiny for what seems now the most absurd of reasons. Some crews would not sail past the point of Africa for fear of turning black. Others were distracted when the wind held for days together while they were outward bound, lest

The red hulled Prince Shoal lightship
stands sentinel at the Saguenay's mouth.

it might never blow the other way in North America and so they would not be able to get back home."

Jacques Cartier was a master mariner whose home was at St. Malo, in Brittany. There are some who hint that he may have been a corsair. It is a swashbuckling suggestion, and hints at a colorful story that we must reluctantly forego, for Jacques Cartier seems to have been too accurate a surveyor, too keen a recorder of his travels to have been of the pirate kin. He sailed, as Norman and Breton fishermen do to this day, all the way across the Atlantic without the aid of navigating instruments, or even chart or compass, steering by the stars and trusting to the instinct which his sea-faring ancestry bequeathed to him. Already the sailors were awed by the immensity of the Gulf. At any moment they expected to turn a point and come upon some fabulous oriental city. What they might meet with there they could only guess at in their simple minds. At last they came to these twin walls brooding over this slit in the earth. Here surely were the portals to another world.

Cartier was, you will remember, a simple mariner, without rank or learning. We have accumulated a lot of learning in the four hundred years that have passed since his day, and if we could strip ourselves of it, even in imagination, we could conceive the magnificent courage of this man who dared so much of the unknown. Cartier fell in with the painted savages of this country with a mind already prepared for marvels, so he misinterpreted much that they had to say. Beyond the portals, he believed them to say, lay the Kingdom of the Saguenay. Far up was a fabulous white race that wore woollen cloth and did not eat. Treasure trove lay in the river, rocks rich in rubies and emeralds and amethysts, waiting to be gathered up by the daring.

But Cartier was more of an explorer than a treasure hunter, so he turned back into the St. Lawrence and sailed on up to Quebec.

One thing and another kept the Saguenay a place of mystery until a hundred years ago. Even then the Indians were reluctant to tell what they knew of their hunting grounds. The government organized a commission to explore and survey the district and find out what the truth really was. So little indeed was known of the region that the commissioners were actually looking for a volcano somewhere on the north shore. The report which they made was the basis on which the future development of this corner of the Dominion has rested.

Even mundane business enterprise, when it did come

Three Basque traders in a Saguenay
bay two centuries ago.

111

here, took on something of the romantic. It was during the wars with Napoleon that England was cut off from the Scandinavian timber markets, and, being in need of supplies for the navy, she sent out to Canada a young man named William Price, to search for suitable material. What young Price saw of the country then impressed him so much that when the war was over he came out here to settle. He soon realized how rich the Saguenay country was in timber, and eventually he went to the little mission and trading town of Chicoutimi and began work. He became the veritable Father of the Saguenay, a king of the timber trade, and the founder of a dynasty which still flourishes. The house of Price is a Canadian family of proud and romantic traditions. William Price established thirty industrial centres in the Saguenay country and left fourteen children behind him when he died in 1867, the year of Confederation. He opened up a country as large as a continental kingdom to the use of modern Canada.

The timber business has preserved for the country something of its primeval qualities. The cutting of timber has raised a race of woodsmen, the natural successors of the trappers and hunters. And in the wake of the timber cutters came settlers. The French Canadian timber cutter has pioneered many a patch of Can-

113

ada, put his family upon the land from which the roots of old trees have had to be torn with tireless and prolonged efforts. They have been patient, frugal, contented, in this puny effort to conquer forest lands and turn them to fields and meadows.

If Louis Hémon had delayed his coming to Canada until to-day we would never have had his book *Maria Chapdelaine* to immortalize the pioneers of the Saguenay and Lake St. John districts. To-day Louis Hémon might have fallen in with settlers grimly awake to the dollars-and-cents value of every acre of land, imbued with the new money-lust that comes to every land when it reaches the stage of industrial development. The land that Hémon knew as the raw north yielding stubbornly inch by inch to a hardy race of soil-loving men and women is almost gone. To-day it is a land of colossal enterprises, of mushroom towns, of mighty dams and power houses, mills, factories and railways. To the other mysteries of the Saguenay country has been added the mystery of the ticker and board room. The explorer and trapper yields his adventure to those who sit about the mahogany tables of Montreal, Toronto, London and New York.

When *Maria Chapdelaine* appeared most Canadians, even when they realized the classic simplicity and power

A pulpwood cargo.

of the tale, resented the thought that life so close to home could be so bald, so terrifying. But to-day Peribonka, where Hémon, the "Frenchman from France", found the setting for his tale, is just another village on a motor road that encircles Lake St. John, and the magnificent Peribonka River, with its mad torrents, its rocky pools and white cascades, is not merely a river of beauty but a river of power.

The history of the Saguenay in the white man's era runs something like this,—fish, fur, timber and power. Fish brought the first adventurers here, while under the French régime fur was the lodestone; the Price family came for timber, and in the country they laid bare the twentieth century, set the leaping rivers to work and brought factories to the very banks on which for unrecorded centuries only the noiseless moccasin had trodden.

VII

TADOUSSAC

TADOUSSAC has perhaps the most picturesque situation of any village in Canada. As the ship glides in toward the quay we see the big summer hotel, like a great red and white manor-house, near the shore, the tiny red and white Indian chapel, the stone parish church with its pointed spire, and beyond them, clambering up the sandy slopes of the mamelons, are the houses of the seven hundred or so people who have come to make Tadoussac their home.

The bay at Tadoussac is a lovely pool of water lying within a smooth beach curving like a golden sickle between the two rocky headlands standing guard at the entrance.

Let your imagination strip Tadoussac of its modern village and re-create it as it was in the days gone by. Beyond the yellow beach the land rises in great terraces not of rock, but of sand. There is an Indian tradition that this was the first of the world to emerge upon the face of the waters, and that each of these terraces marks

Tadoussac Wharf.

a dropping of the sea as the earth took shape. When you climb these terraces you will find them as soft and fine as a sea beach.

They were known to the Indian as Mamelons, or the Place of the Great Sands, for these sand hills rise a thousand feet above the water.

The Bay was a favorite rendezvous for Indian tribes, from time immemorial. Here have been fought terrific battles between opposing tribes or confederations of red men. The Iroquois, now reduced to a few thousands and segregated on reserves under white man's sway, were deadly and marauding foes, who travelled incredible distances to make war upon their enemies. The Montagnais and their neighbors in this part of the world, were, in comparison with the Iroquois, a gentle, goodnatured people, fond of fun and laughter, living perhaps nearer to the principle of individualism than any people before or since. They had practically no government, except a certain toleration for a leader here or there who did what little there was in the way of inter-tribal relations. They were true children of nature, with no fixed abode, no possessions except what they could pack into their canoes, trusting to fate for food and clothing and warmth in this land so rich in game. The Montagnais were an imaginative people,

121

and every rock and stream had its legend and its tradition.

The Indians believed it was at this place of golden sands that the red race and the white first came into contact, at a time far beyond our recorded history. Even before the Norsemen, so says legend, men from the lost continent of Atlantis, came here for fish and furs.

Be that as it may, it was four hundred years ago that our authentic history began with Cartier here. There is a memorial to Cartier in Quebec which will show you what this wind beaten sailor was like when he came to Tadoussac. He must have thought it a welcome change from the rocky north shore he had regarded as God's heritage to Cain, so bleak it seemed to him. This was the first kindly harbour, this place "between high mountains of naked rock". But even Tadoussac could not hold him while he sought the capital of Cathay.

Cartier's stories of jewel hordes up the Saguenay prompted Jean François de la Roque, Sieur de Roberval, to plan a settlement on the Saguenay. Francis the First, King of France, granted him letters patent for his enterprise. Cartier was associated with him. As they could get no volunteers for their settlement the King gave them their choice of the convicts condemned to death

122

G. A. Cuthbertson

In 1628 an English fleet under
David Kirke put in to Tadoussac Bay.

123

in the prisons of France. "We need not regard all such persons as degraded criminals," says Professor Wrong in his *Rise and Fall of New France*. "Men were then sent to death for even minor lapses and heresy was deemed an offense as vile as treason. None the less, condemned criminals were not the best material for France's first attempt at colonization. We have glimpses of gangs of prisoners chained together marching under guard to St. Malo. Women as well as men were to go and we hear of a girl of eighteen chained to a hideous wretch whom she was to marry."

The plan failed, but Roberval did try to sail the Saguenay and lost one small ship and eight of his men there, in his search for rubies and emeralds. One strange tale remains to us of that expedition. Roberval was a harsh and greedy man, and when he sailed he brought with him his ward, a lovely young niece, who, during the voyage fell in love with a gentleman of the party. Roberval brutally attempted to put an end to the affair and when Marguerite defied him, he put her off his ship onto the Isle of Demons in the Gulf of St. Lawrence along with an old Norman nurse. Her lover strapped his musket to his back, jumped over board from the retreating vessel and joined her.

The following year Marguerite had a child, born on

125

that unfriendly island. But the tiny thing died. So did the old peasant nurse. So did the man. Only frail Marguerite lived on in spite of cold and loneliness, killing wild animals and fishing in the sea for her food. Two years afterwards she was rescued by a fishing boat and taken back to France.

It is estimated that by 1600 a thousand vessels crossed the Atlantic every year to fish in American waters, and many of them found their way to Tadoussac. But because the fashions of the times demanded beaver hats for the ladies and gentlemen of the courts, there was a keen new rivalry for furs. In 1599 François Grave, Sieur du Pont, and Pierre Chauvin brought out colonists in an attempt to found a colony at Tadoussac. Again these recruits came from the prisons, and again the effort failed, for the poor wretches that were left to huddle together in the cold at Tadoussac did not know how to live on their own resources. Chauvin came out to Tadoussac for three years and on his last trip he died there.

Another ship dropped anchor in the Bay in 1603. With it begins the real history of New France. On its decks stands the first significant figure in our history, Samuel de Champlain, having his first look at the sav-

"Tadoussac has perhaps the most
picturesque situation of any village
in Canada."

ages who paddled out on the water to encircle the ship and watch it curiously.

Champlain was the first white explorer with the courage to push on up the Saguenay to Chicoutimi. We can imagine him sharing a birch bark canoe, paddled by feathered and painted savages up the salty waters between the astonishing cliffs, marvelling, exclaiming, jotting down notes for his map-making, thrilled to his adventurous soul by the hope that at the end of this strange river he might at last come upon the glory of the oriental cities.

Five years later when Champlain founded Quebec, the fur trade at Tadoussac came within an inch of costing Champlain his life. Among his colonists was one, Jean du Val, who had plotted with the Basques at Tadoussac to murder Champlain and to sell the camp at Quebec to the enemy fur traders. Most of Champlain's party were in the plot, but when one loyal servant revealed it to him, Champlain took stern measures. Jean du Val was executed and his head set upon a pike in the infant camp at Quebec.

In 1615, Champlain brought out to New France the first missionaries, the gentle Recollets. Father Dolbeau, one of the heroes of the Saguenay, came to Tadoussac to attempt to instil into the two or three thou-

127

9

sand nomadic savages the principles of Christian doctrines. Two years later we find another Recollet, Father Paul Huet, trying to say mass at an open air shrine, while two sailors from a French trading ship waved branches of a fir tree around him to ward off the mosquitoes from his face and hands while he performed his holy office.

Next came Father LeCaron, who lived four years with the Indians, nearly smoked into blindness in their teepees or frozen to death on the trails, loathing their filthy ways, yet determined to teach them the ways of his faith. An Indian named Choumin had such admiration for the Father that he insisted upon having his first born son christened by Father LeCaron.

Every ship that crossed from France stopped at Tadoussac. Into the little bay sailed galleons and galleys, high pooped, carved and painted, fighting ships and merchant ships, and ships loaded to the decks with stores for the Indian trade.

Here, one day in 1620, a great ship with sagging sails and buffeted hull slid in to rest. Every man from the trading post went out eagerly to meet her while stolid savages drifted near her in the Bay. Then, to everyone's amazement, a fair head peered over the gunwales, a young, golden-haired woman with eyes as blue as the skies. This was Hélène Boulle, the first gentle-woman to cross to New France, with her husband, the good Sieur de Champlain. She is searching the bobbing canoes for a familiar face and suddenly she finds it. Frantically she waves her handkerchief to attract his attention while Etienne Boulle, her brother, sees her for the first time with amazement.

There is a romantic interest attaching to the association between Tadoussac and the three handsome young brothers, David, Lewis and Thomas Kirke, who in 1629 captured Quebec and took Champlain prisoner.

There were two young kings on the thrones of France and England. Charles of England married Princess Henrietta Marie of France, so the two young sovereigns became brothers-in-law. But Henrietta brought with her to England only half of her "dot", and Louis was exceedingly reluctant to pay over the rest of it. The family quarrel led to war and Charles was only too glad to give letters of marque to the three young Englishmen who wanted to sail out and take Quebec. The unfortunate thing about it, for the Kirke boys, was that before they had a chance to accept the keys of starving Quebec, the brothers-in-law had made up their quarrels and the conquest was automatically valueless.   129

The Kirkes made two trips to Tadoussac. In 1628 they captured so many French ships and had so much loot and so many prisoners that they could not ascend to Quebec, so they came back again in 1629. Having had no supplies from France, Quebec was starving. David stayed at Tadoussac and sent Lewis and Thomas up to Quebec, where, in a very nicely worded letter, they told Champlain that they intended to have Quebec and they would much prefer not to put him to too much inconvenience; would he be good enough to hand over the fort without fighting, and they were his affectionate servants.

Champlain being wise and humane, took the more discreet course and surrendered the city. The brothers were the soul of courtesy to the older gentleman. They would not enter his rooms at the fort, nor interfere with his personal belongings. They were Protestants, their mother being a French Huguenot, and they not only permitted mass but they supplied the wine for it, the colonists having none.

About two thirds of the colonists now decided to return to France, so with the priests and Champlain with them, the English sailed back to Tadoussac where all the ships were to be mustered for the return to England.

At Tadoussac the quarrels between the Catholics

130

and Huguenots grew hot and bitter. Indeed, one of
the officers of the Kirkes, a certain Jacques Michel, grew
apoplectic over the arguments, and died there. The
Kirkes proceeded to give him the noblest funeral that
Tadoussac had seen or has seen since. A coffin was made
for him on which was laid a drawn sword. Marine
officers carried it to his lonely grave and two hundred
men from the ships marched behind in tribute to a
brave officer. The Huguenot minister repeated the
prayers of the reformed church over him, that probably
being the only Protestant burial service ever heard at
Tadoussac. All the ships were called from their anchor-
ages thereabouts and lay in the Bay, and after the
musket volley, ninety guns from the ships barked their
requiem to the dead adventurer.

For a while the trading rights at Tadoussac were
auctioned off every year, but after 1675 it became one
of the chief trading posts of the King's Domain and
its profits went to add splendor to the court of Ver-
sailles, to buy silver chairs and glittering crystal candel-
ebra for a monarch whose extravagant love of luxury
knew no equal.

Under the British régime Tadoussac became one of
the posts of the North-West Company, founded by
those romantic Scottish merchants of Montreal who

wrote a new page in the story of trade and exploration. It finally became a Hudson's Bay Company trading post when the two fur companies amalgamated.

I came upon a curious old man at Tadoussac, a small, thin old chap whose parchment-like skin hung upon his bones. He walked with a cane and talked picturesque and toothless English, but he told me that he was born in Tadoussac nearly ninety years ago and that his father's home and the home of the factor of the Hudson's Bay company were the only houses there. His grandfather was a deserter from an English frigate about the year 1812 or so. He married a French girl at Baie St. Paul and years later was engaged to command a fur trading schooner for the fur company. His grandson, this old Alfred Hovington, remembered the time when three hundred Montagnais families came down the Saguenay every June, to camp and trade at Tadoussac for the summer. The rocky point where the ship lands, called L'Islet, was the spot where they built their bark teepees and around the little cove beyond it they turned up their canoes. Around the golden sands of Tadoussac Bay they danced their old tribal dances, while enormous fires blazed and threw their red lights against the shield of woods upon the bluffs.

In all these years Tadoussac was never a village. It

132

A Glimpse of the past—a Huguenot
trader outward bound from the Saguenay.

was a vivid trading post in the summer time, a deserted, desolate patch of land for the rest of the year. It was only with the passing of the Hudson's Bay Company's rights and the coming of the timber merchants, and after them the summer visitors that Tadoussac became a settlement. That is why you find no old habitant homes in Tadoussac, no traces of the old-established feudal traditions of the St. Lawrence settlements.

VIII

SINGING PINES AND SHINING WATERS

THERE is another Tadoussac beside the Tadoussac of the trader and priest, it is the Tadoussac of the summer visitor, that cheery, sunny, fascinating colony that seems a bit of another world. There are plenty of greybeards of to-day who remember when they played as children in these sands before it was "discovered" long ago as an ideal summer place.

July and August are the popular months for Tadoussac though there are those wise enough and lucky enough to spend June and September there, too. There is an elixir in the air of Tadoussac that defies description. In Tadoussac you feel that you have an abundance of life that you seldom have elsewhere. It pulses through your veins and lightens you upon your feet until you feel that rocks were merely made to be danced over.

You may sit around the Bay and watch the white whales play and realize the spirit that seems to animate them. You love their lazy grace, as they twist and

136

White painted lighthouses are
perched at frequent locations on the
precipitous banks below Murray Bay.

turn, playing about in the pure joy of existence and you don't wonder at all why they all come to Tadoussac. They have little fear of all the summer visitors for they plunge and roll far inside the Bay even when the ship is docking at the quay. And sometimes while you watch the white whales at play you see some sleek black heads popping up here and there, in two and threes and fours, for the seals, too, love Tadoussac. They crawl out of the water and sun themselves on the rocks at the mouth of the Saguenay and make an occasional excursion into the Bay to make sure that everything goes well with Tadoussac.

If you need any proof that this air is different from any other air, other than the intangible proof of well-being, just see the marigold beds around the Hotel Tadoussac. Never were there marigolds such as these, of such a circumference, of such feathery texture or of so many shades of gold. Here they are in creamy yellow, with the petals tipped on the outside with flame, so that as you move the blossoms in your hands they have an iridescent quality. Others are tawny gold, and others still deepest orange. The zinnias here are big upstanding fellows, too, nasturtiums are defiantly gay, and there are other flowers to bring joy or

139

envy to the heart of any gardener; but the marigolds, sea kissed, are of a very special Tadoussac breed.

Every morning at Tadoussac is a challenge. The days never seen long enough or numerous enough to do all those things that one finds to do in a holiday in the open. There are innumerable walks about the environment of Tadoussac. First of all there is Dwight Park, overlooking the Bay to the east. To reach it you walk past the parish church to the main village street, turn to your right and the road will presently bring you to the golf links on one side and the entrance to Dwight Park on the other. This little park, given for the pleasure of future generations of peace-seekers at Tadoussac, is a place of perfumed pine and spruce and cedar trees, with little paths running here and there, to viewpoints from which the water and the hills beyond may be seen. It is deeply carpeted with scented pine needles that have fallen for uncounted summers on the rocks. Perhaps if you lie down here with your head on your arms and lazily watch the patches of blue that are so strangely patterned with tree branches, moving in the winds above you, you may be scolded for your intrusion by a saucy red squirrel who will chatter importantly as he scurries up a tree trunk and selects a branch that will bring him over your head. There, behind the shield of pine sprays he will watch you with his bright eyes and storm and scold like a little sergeant-major.

After you have wandered about Dwight Park you may continue up the sandy road, deep rutted, twisty and silent. Under the trees you will find a sign, "Danger, speed eight miles" and you will smile in sophisticated recollection of six o'clock traffic jams at home. This road leads you on toward the picturesque park lands where so many delightful summer homes have been built, some of them in the old French-Canadian cottage style. Or it will lead you farther on to marvel at the patience and tenacity and success of the settlers who have chosen to be farmers on this far-away rocky north shore.

.   .   .   .

The headland to the eastward of the Bay shuts off the view of the St. Lawrence but the shore beyond is a place of curious contours, of surprising little coves and rocks of glorious color. If you go far enough you come to high clay cliffs, furrowed and sculptured by rains and storms into amazingly fantastic shapes. Follow the sandy beach to the headland at low water and you may walk comfortably along the tide-washed rocks and sand, but if the tide is in you may make your way with only pleasurable effort over the rocks.

141

There are magnificent bits of scenery here. Sunset floods the cracked and furrowed ancient rocks with superb color, wakens them as if with a wand of flame. Here, too, you may see very plainly Lark Point, the low-lying land on the other side of the Saguenay where Champlain made a treaty with the Indians to support them against the Iroquois. There, though you would not suspect it now, in its lonely serenity, was then enacted a dramatic incident upon which rested the fate of the whole future of North America. As a result of that alliance made with the northern Indians against the Iroquois, Champlain, and all Frenchmen after him, earned the undying enmity of the Iroquois. They attached themselves to the English and became their loyal friends through every crisis of North American history. They harried and worried the French colonies for many years, and in any situation where there was a choice to be made they threw in their weight with the English against the French. To-day the remnant of the Six Nations Iroquois live near Brantford in Ontario, where they settled at the close of the Revolution when they again clung to the British standard.

There is a tiny village on the west side of the Saguenay, the village of St. Catherine. This at sunset takes on a strange quality, seen from the eastern shore. It

"The ships dance and twist
in fantastic reflections."

10

looks like a toy village set on a stage. All its white gables face west with geometrical precision, and by some strange quality of the evening light, the lonely little settlement is focussed with photographic distinctness, looking as though it was a little bewitched town under a spell, with perhaps a Sleeping Beauty of the Saguenay waiting to be kissed into life.

During his visit to Canada Rupert Brooke came to Tadoussac. That strangely inspired young Englishman came out alone to this shore, and sat gazing with entranced eyes at the great portals of the Saguenay. Rupert Brooke, handsome as an Adonis who had strayed out of Greece into the modern world, was a celebrated swimmer. The waters here tempted him. He stripped and plunged from a rock into the river. Perhaps he had forgotten that the waters of the Saguenay are neighbors of the Arctic. Perhaps he had not dipped a tentative toe into the ripples on the sand. Be that as it may, he stayed only long enough to discover that there were currents from the St. Lawrence with more mercy than those to be found in the cold Saguenay stream,—and that did not take long,—before he raced out of the stinging waves and craved comfort from the sun.

This headland was called by Champlain, Devils' Tower Point, but to-day it has the sober name of Cow's Point. 145

If you have courage for a dip into the salt waters of the Saguenay you may pride yourself upon your adventure, but for pleasure you will probably join the others who swim in a little jewel of a lake, secreted back of the town. You get to it by again passing the parish church, and turning to the left until you come to the little Anglican church set demurely among the pine trees and with a fringe of raspberry bushes beside its gateway. Across the street you will come to a hole in the fence which leads to a trail with the flavor of the swimming-hole route. Beyond the trees, rimmed around with tree-covered hills, you find the lake, with its frame of silver sands, where you may disport yourself with something of the spirit of the white whales.

The children love this lake and dream of its magic when they have gone back to the bondage of the schoolroom in September.

And speaking of school rooms, there is the little village convent which still has something of the air of a summer camp. It is next door neighbor to the hotel, and was founded in a summer cottage. It has been extended now, of course, for the seven young Franciscan Sisters, young French girls from other St. Lawrence villages, have forty boarders and a hundred and sixty day students to look after.

Isle aux Coudres ketches are
among the few sailing vessels
left on the river.

147

These Sisters love their work at Tadoussac, in spite of their poverty and the economic struggle to make all ends meet. They find moments, however, to peer out of their little dormer windows at primrose sunrises and crimson sunsets, and even at silvery moonlit evenings, for they make time between their prayers and their labors to rest their eyes upon changing colors and the unchanging hills around and beyond Tadoussac.

I saw the Sisters one crisp September day out with their charges on the open ground before the parish church, just across the street. It was the first day of school. Two hundred reluctant boys and girls were being marshalled for another year's reading, 'riting and 'rithmetic. I could see that they were puzzled. They would shift this lad from his place to another, then stand back and view the effect with coifed heads tipped to one side. Last June, it seems, each had known his place in the line and fallen into it obediently. But there, what a difference a summer in the sun makes! They have grown into all sorts of lengths, and last spring's sorting will not answer for September. Alphonse, there, walked ahead of Jean in June, his lanky black head coming no higher than Jean's eyebrow. But now, well, Alphonse has stretched. So has Jean. But Alphonse has stretched more than Jean, and to Jean's mortification he must walk ahead of Alphonse. Alphonse gloats and whispers taunts. Eh! bien! after four o'clock Jean will see who has the tallest punch! What feuds, what jealousies are brewing at the moment! What may not an inch mean in Tadoussac where all other things are equal!

Since Tadoussac faces south and is ringed about with hills, it is shut off from a view of the sunset. However, a few steps from the hotel is a ridge of sea-washed rocks facing the western sky. To find it you walk toward the dock, but instead of turning down along L'Islet, you walk straight on across the rocks toward the cottage overlooking the Saguenay. This was once the old pilot house, but it has been converted to a summer cottage and is surrounded with flower beds where orange lillies, larkspur and purple poppies grow. Beyond the house you keep to your left and here you face the stage upon which the daily drama of sunset is played.

The newest development of the theatre is the light drama, where the play of color, of light and of motion, produce emotional effects more tense than the effects of sound. Yet here in the theatre of the Saguenay the drama of light has been played for untold centuries of time. To sit here upon the rocks, or to float in a canoe at the mouth of the Saguenay in the sunset hour is to be transported into a world of glorious and fleeting color pictures. Here against the vast canvas of the sky the sun plays upon the hills and headlands so that the emotions even of the veriest tripper are hushed into reverence and expectancy. Even the grey rocks take on tints of ethereal beauty, haunting shades of amethyst creep up against the greens of the trees.

No one dares predict what an evening will bring forth. It may be an evening of tenuous rags of clouds along the horizon behind which the sun turns slowly to a molten crimson that reflects itself in the basin until the whole glows and shimmers like a crucible. The light will then flood upwards to stain the clouds with rose and cyclamen against a blue sky. Then the rocks flush and their reflections on the water are purple as ripe grapes. Moment by moment the light changes in an unbelievable pageantry, and then retreats as slowly, as magnificently, into the neutrality of dusk.

Just where you left the roadway to go in search of the sunset you come upon a picturesque little cove that is worth exploring. Here is a row of crazy little houses made of all sorts of things, driftwood, old boxes, ship's timbers. They are unpainted, weather stained, picturesque. They all face into the cove on one fantastic little walk, built up on a cribwork, rotting and hap-

151

hazard, that is intended to keep the high tides from washing up to their doorsteps. At one house there is a handful of earth between the door and the cribwork extravagantly abloom with stunted hollyhocks, purple poppies and anything else that can find room to push its way up into the sunlight. On the door rail sits a tame black crow watching the road with a sinister eye.

This little cove is a natural drydock. At low tide it is dry, with only one exit, a narrow passage between the rocks that ring it round. Through this narrow gate come old ships to rot and disappear, or else to out-sail new schooners that came to birth here and feel the springy lift of sea water for the first time in the Saguenay. Here there now lies an old black hulk, its gallant days all done, dreaming of the lash of crested waves and the wild caress of the winds in its topsail. In the sand half-buried, as though in a desecrated grave, is yet an older ship, one perhaps that carried rich bales of furs from the trading posts in Labrador in the days of the Hudson's Bay company. And between them, half fashioned, is another, a new schooner. But the days of activity have left Tadoussac and its builders are careless of time. It will not sail this year. Next year,—perhaps.

A Tramp steamer, the tireless,
patient pack mule of the sea.

IX

THE INDIAN CHAPEL

I T IS a very modest and demure little place, the Indian chapel at Tadoussac, with its red roof and its snowy walls, its tiny turret and its old iron-hinged door, and yet it has about it something that compels both curiosity and affection. White picket fences crawl down the hillside and meet at its steps. Within the rails in tangled grass and bushes stand scores of dark crosses, weather-stained, leaning forlornly this way and that. And when you enter you find a little temple, with narrow, straight-backed pews, tiny framed Stations of the Cross upon the walls, pictures dark with age, and a carved and decorated altar.

This is all that remains of material things to connect the Tadoussac of to-day with the Tadoussac of those adventurous times when the *fleur de lys* still floated over Canada and when the brown-frocked missionaries and the husky fur-traders shared the trails of the Saguenay country.

The Jesuits, who worked at Tadoussac for a hundred and forty odd years, were men of red blood, daring all for the propagation of their faith, men oftentimes of noble or aristocratic birth, of keenly creative minds, who, even in the wilderness, found much on which to whet their intellects. *The Jesuit Relations,* the reports of the missionaries to their Superior in France, are amazing documents, and remain our greatest source of details of those days. These brave soldiers of the Cross made their hampering garments no excuse for avoiding long and tedious journeys, for they were great woodsmen, and tireless travellers, who paddled and preached with equal dexterity. They loved greatly and they died greatly.

So we find them studying anatomy on the bodies of their slaughtered game, dissecting by the smoky flame of a torch, or jotting down botanical notes, or making a record of ethnological observations, translating Indian myths and legends, and sometimes admitting that they believed the redmen had communication with the Devil.

For many years the Jesuits had no permanent mission station at Tadoussac, going there only in the summer with the hunters and travelling with them in the winters in the interior. Father Jean Duquen, from Amiens,

in France, was the first to build a permanent chapel
here. The first building was of cedar, built by the sailors of a French ship, and fragrant it must have been
with the natural perfume of the woods mingling with
the incense. The Duchesse d'Augillon, niece of the
Great Cardinal, Richelieu, gave him the money to
build the chapel, the King gave him a bell to hang in
its turret, and he had drugget of a curious weave
to hang upon the walls. The Duchesse was the
favorite niece of Richelieu, and one of his many relatives
enriched and ennobled by him, and there was a time
when he toyed with the idea of making her Queen of
France. She founded the Hotel Dieu at Quebec, the
oldest hospital in America. The bell still hangs over
the chapel of to-day, and when you hear its thin voice
when it is rung sometimes of a summer afternoon, you
are listening to the same call that rang out into the
wilderness three centuries ago to call the savages to hear
the story of the Christ of Bethlehem. As for the drugget on the walls, the Indians had never seen anything
like it, and they thought the design of the weaving was
some sort of magic spell.

There must have been a sort of barbaric splendor
about the little chapel. Sometimes the painted converts
brought skins as gifts to the missionaries, to be ex-

changed for ornaments for the altar. There is still a crucifix there that was purchased with beaver skins. There were men and women, too, up the St. Lawrence and over in France, who kept an affectionate watch over the chapel and sent it gifts. Everyone who came or went from New France knew Tadoussac and its chapel. Dozens of ladies stitched daintily at silks and linens, making altar cloths and sacerdotal robes for the priests. The nuns at Quebec and the wife of Governor d'Ailleboust mended them and made artificial flowers for the altar. Nuns from far away France sent them statues, crucifixes and rosaries. Madamoiselle Bazire, whose father was once in charge of the trade at Tadoussac, worked for twenty years on embroideries for the chapel.

In the chapel to-day you may see the little, crudely carved candle sticks made by the first missionaries for their altars, and these are among the most touching relics that have survived the long years. In the year after the chapel was built Madame de la Peltrie, the founder of the Ursuline convent in Quebec, came down to Tadoussac to stand as godmother to some Indian girls, the first ceremony of its kind to take place here.

In the sixteen-sixties, when all New France was in mortal fear, the Iroquois swooped down the St. Lawrence and massacred all they could find at Tadoussac and pillaged and burned what there was of a settlement. For years afterwards the Indians would not return to trade or worship there.

The Jesuits were more than missionaries, they were diplomats and map makers, scouts and emissaries. It was in 1671 that Father Albanel, who had spent many years at the mission post, heard from the hunters that there was an English ship on the Sea of the North. Albanel promptly sent word of it to Intendant Talon. Nothing could have been more disturbing to the ears of that handsome and energetic gentleman. He had great ambitions, and among them was the hope to oust the English from America, even from the New England colonies. So, to hear that they had already arrived in the North as well was too much.

The truth was that two Frenchmen, badly treated by the administrators of New France, had gone to England, and revealed there the wealth of the fur trade of the far north. Their tale was so colorful and so convincing that no less a person than the cousin of the King, Prince Rupert, decided to go into the fur business. The English gentlemen who joined him under a charter from the king, were known as the Gentlemen Adven-

11

turers of England. It was one of their ships that the Montagnais hunters had seen.

Intendant Talon sent post haste back to Tadoussac for Father Albanel, and after a consultation at Quebec the priest got just what he wanted most, official support for a journey of adventure up through the north in search of the northern sea which none of the Frenchmen had yet seen. Two other Frenchmen went with him, and a party of Indians. They left one day in August, of 1671, travelled by the Saguenay, Lake Kenogami, to Lake St. John, and at its northern side they camped for the winter with the Indians. This was a country the priest knew well for he had seen as many as twenty savage tribes camped there at one time. In the following summer they went on, discovered Lake Mistassini and came finally to Rupert River and so on down to James Bay. This was the first overland journey to the salt water of Hudson Bay. Here they discovered an English post from which they hauled down the flag and substituted the *fleur de lys*, and while they waited for the return of the English traders, Father Albanel baptised two hundred converts.

They returned at last to Tadoussac, arriving there a year, to the day, from the time of their departure. They had travelled twenty-two hundred miles, encoun-

Isle Aux Coudres Ketch.

tered four hundred rapids and crossed two hundred portages, though their travelling time was exactly sixty-three days.

In the following year Father Albanel returned to the Indians at James Bay, but he was taken prisoner by the English and carried to England where he was detained for three or four years. Twenty years later he died at Sault Ste. Marie, still in pursuit of souls to save.

The little chapel at Tadoussac as it stands to-day is due to Father Claude Godefroy Coquart, who was born at Calais. He was a very busy and efficient gentleman with the keenest interest in everything that went on in his gigantic parish which stretched from the St. Lawrence away to the Arctic. The year in which he was to build the new chapel he was delayed in getting down from Chicoutimi "partly because I wished to conclude a marriage upon which I had set my heart." So he hurried on from his pleasant little match-making episode to the mouth of the Saguenay. It was the Intendant at Quebec who had given him the money for the new chapel and perhaps the timber came down from Chicoutimi, for there was a mill there. On May 16, 1747, Father Coquart himself, adding a little ceremony to the undertaking, drove the first nail and blessed the site. The building was to be ready for the coming of the Indians in June. The funds, however, ran out and the roof had to be left to the beneficence of the next Intendant, François Bigot, of whom we hear so little that is pleasant. Bigot was a grafter and a philanderer and many other things, but this is one good deed that can be set down to the credit side of his account.

However, it was Intendant Hocquart who was the real benefactor of the Indian chapel, and Father Coquart promised in return that on every St. Anne's day there would be a mass in the chapel for his sake. Thereafter, on St. Anne's day, true to the promise, a service of intercession and remembrance was held. The tiny chapel could not hold all who came to worship. Its doors stood open to the world. Below, on the sands were gathered the Indians in their buckskins and feathers. Beyond, some of them floating motionlessly in their canoes, their faces lifted to the mystery under the peaked roof. Beyond them again, at anchor, swung the trading ships from France. To this very day the service on St. Anne's day continues, and the little church, called like a ghost from its silence and solitude, hears mass celebrated at its historic altar and once more the doors stand open to the crowds below while the prayers are offered for the soul of its benefactor.

The tiny Stations of the Cross in the chapel are

the smallest in America and are now a rare set of old prints. In the Vestry behind the church are many fine old vestments, with historic as well as artistic interest.

One day I called at the little convent up the street to ask if one of the Sisters could tell me the story of these old satins and brocades. The request caused a little furore in the even tenor of the day. There was a consultation with the Superior and presently a young nun came out into the little shining parlor and, scarcely able to suppress her excitement under her demureness, she told me that she might come with me, if we would wait until a companion could join her. So presently another little nun, as young, as bright-eyed as herself, joined us, and we set out down the street with a great iron key, for it was a day and an hour in which the chapel, usually open to visitors, was closed. It was quite an adventure to the little Sisters for, though they lived within a stone's throw of the chapel, none of their duties had ever called them there, and they fluttered along, with the wind lifting their black veils.

Within the chapel they exclaimed and murmured over the curious relics, the old paintings, especially the one which tradition says came from the church at Grand Pré to which the Acadians were called to hear the edict of Expulsion. They bent with soft words of

165

endearment over the wax doll, in its quaint old robes stitched by the royal hands of Anne of Austria and given to the chapel as a "petit Jesus" by Louis the Fourteenth. And then, in that gentle ecstasy that seems to become the white-coifed women so well, they drew out of long shallow drawers the beautiful vestments, set after set of them, intended for the various festivals of the church. The garments made rich pools of color in the tiny vestry, copes, chasubles, stoles, birettas and more. They were worn, rubbed, mended, some of them, in the service of the altar, but what a tale they told! Here were rare old handwoven cloths, silk and wool, with silk and metallic embroideries, still vibrant with the selfless devotion of the women whose slender fingers had conjured up with needle and thread patterns still so fresh in color.

.   .   .   .

At Tadoussac there has grown up the most beautiful legend of the North Shore, because legend it is though it is told for good honest fact. I tell it, not because it is true in fact, but because it is true in spirit. Instead of being the story of a dispensation of Providence, this is a warm human document, welling up out of the heart of the devoted.

166

Father Labrosse was the last of the Jesuit missionaries at Tadoussac, the twenty-first in order of service. He came in 1766 and served until his death in 1782. He was a man of great capabilities and wide sympathies and he made himself genuinely beloved by all who came in contact with him. During the French régime there was no printing press in Canada, but as soon as the English began to set type at Quebec, Father Labrosse took to writing books, translations of the Gospels, primers, catechisms and so on. His "first editions" are among the most rare and prized of Canadiana to-day and the Archbishop at Quebec is proud to own a primer published by Father Labrosse in 1767.

After long years of service Father Labrosse was ready to meet death, as he had met life, unafraid.

One evening he spent a few hours with the men at the trading post, playing cards, listening to their fiddles and to the old songs. Then he looked at his big watch and stood up to go.

"Goodnight, my friends," he said. "At midnight I shall be no more. You will find me at the altar in the chapel. Pray do not touch me. Go to l'Isle aux Coudres and there find my friend, the priest. He will come to bury me. Adieu."

His friends listened, half in awe, half in scepticism.

So they went on playing cards, reluctant to separate until the end of the day. Softly in the awesome silence of midnight the old bell tolled. Stirred beyond speech they rose and made their way together to the chapel. Upon the altar a flickering candle glowed, and on his knees, in a soft radiance that seemed more than candle light, the old priest knelt, his face hidden as though he had lowered it before a blinding light.

Out in the night the winds wrestled and the trees rocked and groaned. The waters lashed themselves in foam. Yet the father had said, "Go to l'Isle aux Coudres." The bravest of the men went through the darkness to the beach, launched a canoe for what seemed to be certain death. But awe-stricken, they saw the river open in a windless, waveless avenue ahead of them. Borne on by swift and unseen hands, the canoe made the miraculous journey to l'Isle aux Coudres, and when they came near the shore there stood the priest of the parish.

"I have been expecting you," he said. "My good friend, Father Labrosse, is dead."

They say that all the bells in all the villages along the Saguenay and the St. Lawrence had tolled at midnight, rung by unseen hands, for the passing of Father Labrosse.

However, the more prosaic version of the written history of the register tells us that Father Labrosse died like any other man and was buried under his altar at the chapel. But certain it is that the Indians came and flung themselves upon the floor over his grave and talked to him as though he still would heed them. And to-day, the old men of Tadoussac will tell you the legend in good faith. They will show you the marks of his knees and his snowshoes in the rocks and will point out the place where, even after death, he redeemed a promise and returned a silver cup he had borrowed. We need no documentary evidence on the goodness of the man, for be he priest or not, he who stores up enough of sweetness in his lifetime to have it perfume his memory for six generations is well worthy of his legend.

. . . .

When the regime of the Hudson's Bay Company ended and Tadoussac gradually became a village of lumbermen's families, the Indian chapel was used as a parish church. But gradually it fell into very bad shape and in 1880 a group of English people in Montreal raised enough money among themselves to renovate and restore the chapel, and they left it as it is to-day. It was a parish church until 1885 when the congregation moved up the hill to the stone church of to-day.

169

Years afterwards, when an English girl was about
to marry a French husband, she decided that the little
chapel at Tadoussac was just the place for a romantic
wedding. So in all her bridal finery of white satin and
ethereal lace and tulle, she went there to pledge her marriage vows while the priest donned his historic vestments. The bride still comes to Tadoussac and knows
and loves all of the village folks. Many of them remember that wedding day, for it was a red letter day for
the village, and she still boasts with a tender pride that
she was the only bride with white satin and a train and
a veil to be married in the Indian chapel.

X

THE UPPER SAGUENAY AND BEYOND

THE white river ships that sail up the Saguenay leave Tadoussac in the evening, and so it is in the gathering dusk that travellers approach the first great cliffs, to sail, as Jacques Cartier said, "between high mountains of naked rock" up the storied stream. Perhaps the last of the sunset colors are still drenching the skies and against the glow the strange contours of the Saguenay hills stand in Olympian dignity.

Beneath, in the great chasm that repeats these visible contours of the Laurentians, the waters flow on to the sea in the solemn constancy of Nature. Above, the granite pallisades more than double the proportions of the depth beneath. And there, suspended on the face of the waters, we lie in our white ship, a plaything in the midst of all this magnitude.

If you are a fortunate traveller you may have a night of luminous silence, with the sky immeasurably deep and blue when the jewelled heavens seem to come close

171

to the Saguenay. There may even be a moon to tip the hills in silver and brighten the velvet darkness of the deep stream itself.

Morning will find the ship at Bagotville, on Ha! Ha! Bay, named, so it is said, by the explorers who were able to laugh at themselves for having blundered into the Bay when they were in search of the main stream. It is small wonder that they made the error, for the entrance to the Bay is wider than the main stream and the Bay widens to a distance of six miles and is nine miles deep from Cape West to Port Alfred.

It was to Ha! Ha! Bay that the travellers of long ago all came, in order to cross by river, stream and portage to lovely Lake Kenogami, deep as the Saguenay, and leading from its western end into still more streams and portages, to Lake St. John.

It was to the rich alluvial soils around Ha! Ha! Bay that the first colonists came and settled in the village of Grand Baie where there is a memorial to their pioneer heroism. Next door neighbor to Grand Baie is Port Alfred, a mill town, the third of the towns which overlap each other in the curve at the bottom of the Bay.

At Bagotville the big ships of the Canada Steamship Lines have their terminal and if you are bound for Chicoutimi the short journey overland is made by

172

"We sail on one of the white
ships of the river fleet."

173

motor. If you sail in the smallest ship of the fleet, the *Saguenay* which is known among sailors as "a happy ship", you will tie up at the docks of Chicoutimi itself.

If you want to be happy in Chicoutimi, have nothing to say about the rival claims of Bagotville, Port Alfred, Grand Baie, et al, to terminal honors. Chicoutimi is at the foot of the turbulent cascades of the Upper Saguenay, her harbour is limited, but she is making a loyal fight to maintain her maritime honors and expects to be the Montreal of the Saguenay.

Chicoutimi comes from the Cree word Ishkotimew, which means "up here the water is deep". It was to Chicoutimi that William Price came, as his memorial, put up by the people of Chicoutimi, will tell you.

Between Chicoutimi and Lake St. John the Saguenay is not navigable. In seventeen miles the water drops five hundred feet, twice as great as the drop at the Falls of Niagara.

Lake St. John is saucer shaped, round and shallow, and it hoards the tributes of five great rivers and many small ones flowing out of a basin of thirty thousand square miles. All this water leaves the Lake by twin channels that surround Ile d'Alma, the southern channel La Petite Décharge, and the northern channel La Grande Décharge. La Petite Décharge is almost peace-

12

ful compared with the uproarious current of La Grande
Décharge which has been harnessed at the Isle Maligne
power plant to develop 540,000 horse power of elec-
tricity. The reunited streams force their way down the
stone chasm and farther down stream, at Chute à Caron,
they will be made to yield up yet another 800,000 horse
power.

In the great basin of Lake St. John there are many
other power projects to be developed to feed pulp and
paper plants, such as that at Dolbeau, where a whole
new town sprang up over night when the wheels of the
mill began to revolve. Close neighbor to this colossal
mill is the Trappist monastery at Mistassini where for
thirty years men have lived in silence, working their
great farm with agricultural ingenuity, making the
famous Oka cheese, and fasting as long and as often as
their strength will allow; a strange bit of medievalism
in contrast to the life at the mill which is turning out
newsprint to carry the news of this restless world of
ours.

There is a motor road around Lake St. John, a curious drive that leads through the whole scale of life, from
the acquiescence and serenity of the plodding colonists
to the vaulting ambitions of the money kings.

On the roadside you will find many shrines, set up

Up anchor, early morning, at Ha! Ha!
Bay.   A Collier getting ready to go in
to the wharves at Port Alfred.

by faithful hands, one of them, a Christ on the Cross near Desbiens, curiously carved by an ambitious but untrained hand from a single log, but beautiful to the neighbors because of its significance. Desbiens is at the mouth of the Metabetchouan River where the Jesuit missionaries early in their regime in this district, had the first model farm in America. They had an estate here of three hundred acres and grew not only grain and vegetables, but they also had plum trees and fruit bushes as well. Traces of their farmlands were discovered in 1828 by the government exploration commission, even to the marks of their furrows, and ancient gooseberry bushes still survived a generation after the last of them, had garnered their final harvest. These extraordinary men also had a trail from the Metabetchouan to Quebec, over which they drove their cattle to market. Their audacity and energy are almost unbelievable.

Roberval is an important Lake town, where the Ursuline Sisters teach the social graces to daughters of the pioneers. At St. Felicien the road crosses the River Ashuapmouchouan. The parish priest here has a lovely garden of old-fashioned flowers within a white picket fence, and in his study, spread upon the wall behind his desk, is an enormous family chart, made with infinite pains, tracing his ancestry back for a dozen generations to that Louis Hébert, the first farmer at Quebec, where all good French Canadians are well content to stop their genealogical explorations, as though he was the Adam of New France.

The road leads on to Dolbeau where it crosses the fabulous Mistassini, the river of legends, that leads into mighty Lake Mistassini where the Ark of the Indians came to rest and up which Albanel went on his way to Hudson's Bay. It then runs through Peribonka where Louis Hémon found his setting for *Maria Chapdelaine,* meandering along the picturesque banks for miles. Homeward it runs to Chicoutimi past the stupendous dams at Isle Maligne and the thriving town of St. Joseph d'Alma.

One of Chicoutimi's new neighbors, half way to the mill town of Kenogami, is Arvida, a model town built around the plant of the Aluminum Company of Canada which came here for power and imports its raw materials from British Guiana.

To Chicoutimi must go much of the credit for what has been done in securing financial and administrative aid in the establishment of Big Business in the Lake St. John District. It has long since become the aggressive unofficial capital of the district. On the ridge of the hill stands the offspring of the Jesuit mission, the church

A Saguenay saw mill.

vigilant, the Cathedral, the bishop's palace, the convent, hospital, school and seminary. Once an outpost of the mission world, Chicoutimi is rapidly becoming a humming, progressive city. New docks proclaim Chicoutimi's intention to remain a seaport in spite of the reluctance of captains to wrestle with the swift currents of the Chicoutimi channel.

Across from Chicoutimi is the picturesque village of St. Anne, looking as though it had escaped the fever of progress, sprawling sleepily on its rocks.

XI

THE SAGUENAY—THE RIVER OF
DEEP WATERS

THE journey down the Saguenay begins in early morning so that the deep chasm of the Saguenay may be seen by light of day. If you sail from Chicoutimi you slip out from the quay into the currents that have flowed from a thousand valleys of the north and on their way paid tribute to the needs of twentieth century life in the dams and turbines of the Lake St. John country. As the ship sweeps down stream the hilly town of Chicoutimi gradually recedes and the banks begin to assume those rolling masses that characterize the Saguenay Valley. On the north shore little rivers tumble out of the hills and a village clings tenaciously to its rocky perch. This is St. Efulgence one of those isolated settlements where the old French traditions of social life still flourish.

At first thought one may assume that in travelling the Saguenay you are running north or south, but actually, as a geographical fact, the river runs almost east and west. That is merely another misconception of this curious river, of which the Indians said to the white men that it lay in a climate which no white man could endure, describing its hills as snow-capped all the year round. Now we know that the Saguenay country is rich and fertile with half a million acres of cultivated farmlands. The fables are exploded and the land laughs at its legends. Actually Chicoutimi is a hundred miles farther south upon the map than the city of Winnipeg, which would deny any Arctic characteristics.

Certainly, however, these great bald rocks, "without any savor of earth", as an old explorer wrote, do not suggest the agricultural life. Only in an occasional corner, where a river with infinite patience has covered the rocks with soil, do we see a foothold for man. Yet when we do come upon these they beckon and disturb us with their promises of beauty, of unexplored loveliness beyond, of healing solitude and contentment. By their very contrast with the baffling immensity of the Laurentian hills they make their appeal.

Far ahead of the ship looms Cape East, on the north, twin to that Cape West, on the south shore which stands guard at the entrance to Ha! Ha! Bay.

If your vessel has tied up at Bagotville it is here you will begin the descent of the Saguenay.

On the north shore you will presently see the little toy village of Descente des Femmes. Three little coves here break the shore line with small knobs of headlands between them. The village itself crawls lazily up a slope. Descente des Femmes got its name from an Indian tragedy. A tribe of hunters fell upon evil days and advanced slowly to starvation owing to their inherently improvident ways. The Indian squaws, with some curiously unnatural feminine strength, left their husbands to go in search of succor. They travelled desperately along a little river until they came out on the Saguenay at this point where they made their "descente" upon white men and aid.

Here you get the full flavor of pioneer life among men and women who think simply, live frugally and work happily, on fields coaxed from the wilderness. They are great story tellers for they have plenty of winter leisure to develop their talents. They approach a tale slowly, with infinite detail of the subject, particularly if it is of a distant cousin, with a knotty family relationship to be unravelled. They savor the effect of their anecdote and embellish the incident with flourishes to spin its worth as far as possible. They are still sufficiently unique to be fascinating, these kindly pioneers of Descente des Femmes.

On the south shore, as the ship approaches the vicinity of Cape Trinity, there is Le Tableau, or The Blackboard, an enormous face of sheer black rock, hundreds of feet high, looking like a titanic blackboard. Indeed, Arthur Buies, a historian of the Saguenay of fifty years ago, suggests that on its face the chief facts in the story of the Saguenay should be carved in imperishable letters. Opposite to Le Tableau, across the river, is a beautiful bend in the shore which is called Tableau Bay.

At last we are coming to the culmination of the River's magnificence, the supreme effort of Nature's extravagance, the towering cliffs of Capes Trinity and Eternity.

How ineffective words seem in attempting to capture something of the spirit of these mighty rocks. The ship seems an insignificant toy as it creeps close to the granite rocks that soar straight above us, as high as the ramparts of heaven.

In the Bay a silence possesses the world. Trinity stands on the one hand, Eternity on the other, ancient and imperial hills, casting their shadows into the deep pool. Close to two thousand feet Eternity reaches into the sky, putting to shame the loftiest ambitions of human architects. Put Canterbury Cathedral down here at the water's edge, and on its lofty towers pile

Winchester, York, Lincoln, Wells, Westminster, Rochester, and over them all set Salisbury cathedral with its slim and sublime spire, and still you have room for more beneath the dome of Eternity.

Aloof, patched with innumerable colors in the rocks, drenched with warmth in one light, stern and grey in another, or suffused with amethystine shadows in another, these cliffs, that seem almost naked, have to yield place to the persistence of life in this north that seems to be the source of life and energy, for the trees, wind buffeted, hardy, tenacious, take root in seemingly impossible crevices, and lean out triumphantly over the precipitous sides.

Yet here we come in this monumental quietude and blare at the rocks with siren whistles. Almost within hand's reach of the cliffs we seem to be when the whistles shriek impertinently at the sides of Trinity. The rocks seem to give back an echo in greater volume and wild Olympian laughter rolls from cliff to cliff, as the echoes flee from one high point to another, a mighty jest tossed between gods that perhaps still dwell in the splendid isolation of the mountain peaks—"on the hills like gods together, careless of mankind."

And so, having made the Capes stoop to amuse us, we turn out and make an arc in the Bay as we return to

188

mid-stream, to carry away for all time something of the sense of magnitude that they make upon our imagination, even though we have no standard by which to measure them with our eyes.

There is an Indian legend which explains the three gashes in Trinity. The Indians people the air and forests, rocks and rivers, with spirits of good and evil power, and these primitive people were forever depositing tidbits on islands or at the entrances to caves to propitiate their gods. They believed that the soul of a drowned Indian was doomed to haunt the waters where he went down and were forever anxious to keep on friendly terms with the spirits of the streams. Fancy then their dread of this river which is, as Castell Hopkins has said, "able to hold all the fleets of the world, though with hardly a place for anchorage". Cataracts they thought to be the dwelling places of vicious spirits and when the waters of a lake were storm tossed they were stirred by the gods within.

The Mistassinis have a legend of the Flood. They believe that the "big canoe" came to rest on a high and sacred mountain in their country. About it still marches a sentinel, a tall and handsome old Indian with his bow and arrows. On the mountain peak still lie the incorruptible timbers of the legendary craft. So, too, the

189

Indians had their story of the fallen angels. When the Great Manitou had to banish them from heaven he tossed them all down into the Saguenay. All perished in the fall but one, more powerful than the others, who was merely crippled. He was still able to make a lot of trouble. He fought and struggled with the river that held him prisoner and in his rage hoped to do harm to the earth born.

Then one day Mayo, the father of the Indian race, a giant man who could uproot the pine trees as easily as we crop grass on the roadside, came strolling along the Saguenay. He decided to launch his canoe upon the Bay between the great Capes. No sooner was he on the water than it became so agitated that great waves rolled in towards shore. Mayo realized that he had come upon the demon who was bent on possessing him. So he raised a hasty prayer to the Great Manitou and prepared to help himself. As soon as the demon showed himself Mayo seized him by the tail and drew him out of the water. Swinging him in a mighty arc Mayo brought his head down upon the cliff. The rocks split, but the demon did not die. He brought him down again, and again the cliff groaned and showed another gash. But still the demon breathed. With one last tremendous effort Mayo brought the evil head against the granite, and he

190

Ancient and imperial hills, casting
their shadows into the deep pool.

expired. But there was still another breach in the stone. And this explains the contour of Trinity.

To-day as you sail out of the Bay you will see in the rocks below the Virgin a great Indian face in the natural lines of the rock. Whether this is the Great Manitou's memorial to Mayo, or not, we cannot even guess.

But above the Indian face stands the symbol of another faith. As though Trinity had been carved out of chaos as a natural shrine, here has been set a great white figure of the Virgin. There is a benignity about Our Lady of the Saguenay, as she stands high above the river with her hands raised perpetually in prayer for the travellers. As the ship travels up stream at night a search light plays in and out among the pines and rocks in search of her; and suddenly, set in the diffused white light, the figure will come to life with something of the unearthly in its loneliness and remoteness.

But in the sunlight the white figure stands out against the fir trees like an alabaster Madonna in a Gothic shrine.

This, it is said, is the largest Madonna in the world, and it came from the hands of that Louis Jobin who preserved faithfully until death, the traditions of the old Cap Tourmente school of Laval's creating. He was

191

a young man, not much over thirty, when he began this enormous Virgin in his workshop at St. Joachim. He was not famous then, just a good, skillful craftsman, with a sense of adventure, and something of imagination, when he accepted this curious commission. He did not become famous until, when he was old and bent, historians and art collectors suddenly began to search for samples of his work. Few seem to realize that this celebrated Virgin is his. The idea, however, was conceived by Charles Napoleon Robitaille, one of the first commercial travellers on the Saguenay. In winter time the river hereabouts is frozen over, and on one occasion when he was travelling up the ice in a sleigh he ran into a hole and went through. He prayed frantically for aid, and miraculously, as it seemed to him, he found himself, his horse and his sleigh, safely out of the water and on firm ice. He vowed, in thanksgiving for his escape and for his recovery from the long illness that followed his wintry dip, to put a Virgin on the rocks above. So it was that he came to put the task into the hands of Louis Jobin.

The figure was made in three sections, in order to make the task of getting it up on the rocks possible. It was carried by schooner up the river to the foot of Trinity, and then a party of workmen were set to work

192

on the job of cutting a trail through the woods and over the rocks to the selected spot. The men had to build a sort of wooden railway, over which the huge carved blocks could be dragged by block and tackle from ledge to ledge.

After fifty years there still is a link on the Saguenay with that prodigious task, for the First Pilot of the S.S. *St. Lawrence*, Jean Duguay, was one of the men who helped to haul the Virgin to her rocky throne.

The statue is still cared for by the Robitaille family, and kept in excellent condition. The wooden figure is sheathed in lead and frequently painted.

In a quaint little romance written in the '80's by W. H. H. Murray, Trinity is the setting for a mad plunge for life. The romance is written about an old Indian legend which predicted the end of the Lenni-Lenape tribe when a princess of that tribe married a man of pure white blood. According to the story the brother of the chief of the tribe had married, in France, a very beautiful Basque woman, one of that race from Southern Spain which had its origin in lost Atlantis. Because of her descent from the royal line of Atlantis the Basque woman named her only daughter Atla.

In a great battle at Tadoussac, the chief unknowingly killed his brother who had returned to the country and thrown in his lot with the Esquimaux of Labrador. The chief adopted his brother's daughter, and in the tale John Norton, a trader from Tadoussac, is called north to the chief's death bed to receive Atla as his bride. On their journey down to Tadoussac, where their marriage is to take place, Norton and Alta are caught in a great forest fire on the south shore. Making a desperate dash for life the two flee toward the Saguenay banks, and when Alta falls with exhaustion, Norton, carrying her in his arms, continues his race against the flames. He races out of the woods at the top of Trinity, sees the river, dark with smoke, below, and unable to check his wild speed, dashes down from ledge to ledge until he stands on the rim of the precipice that hangs over the river. Then, according to the enthusiastic author, "heaving up his huge frame, still clasping her sweet weight within strong arms, he plunged, like a burnt log rolling out of fire, into the dark, deep, blessed tide."

The scenery hereabouts is wildly romantic and the settings change with every mile as the ship glides on down stream. The water of the Saguenay is never blue. I once asked a Saguenay captain what he thought the elusive color really was. With perfect gravity he assured me that in his opinion it was the color of good

A coasting vessel with a cargo of
lumber, anchors in the twilight.

beer! But there are moments when the sun lifts the river out of this plebeian classification and turns the Saguenay to cloth of gold.

The Saguenay, by the way, was the first middleman's route in America. The Montagnais were quick to learn the benefits of retail trade and when they traded at Tadoussac they bought sufficient stuff from the Basque, or French ships, to carry off to their rendezvous with other Algonquin tribes, there to be traded for furs from the interior, which in turn they traded off next summer at Tadoussac.

The fame of the Saguenay travelled far afield even in those very earliest days of the white man's history in America. It was as far back as 1640 that one day, to the amazement of Quebec, a white man and an Indian guide arrived out of the Chaudière River and crossed the St. Lawrence to Quebec. He was an Englishman and he had come all the way from Mexico, where, he told the Frenchmen, he had heard about the Saguenay. He was about to set off, he said blandly, to travel up the Saguenay in search of the North-West Passage to Asia.

The man was promptly arrested by the French and his only glimpse of the Saguenay was at Tadoussac where his ship called, as he was being carried back to Europe for his impudence.

197

Sometimes one wonders, leaning over these silent and bewitched waters, what tales the river could tell, what secret valleys it has left behind. Sometimes its turbulent waters seem to reach some strange serenity as though the river had its moods and emotions. Over the sides of a canoe, buried fathoms deep, are the clouds that you thought were hung so high above you. Brooding on the rocky edges at sunset, the flaming clouds seem to come floating to one's feet, none of their fire quenched, so still the river lies. And yet again, the winds may race in fantastic glee up and down between the rocks and what was once mirror is whipped into salty spray upon the sea-worn rocks, and it seems as if all the old Indian devils have come back whistling in the bending pines.

Frequently, up and down the river you will come upon little schooners, technically called Isle aux Coudres ketches, with both sails and engines, and looking like floating wood piles. These little vessels, built around the coast and running roughly to a hundred feet in length, carry cordwood and package freight and some-times passengers, to and from the river settlements. They are usually manned by a father and his sons, the mother of the family and her daughters going along with them for the summer transferring the home from

198

Midsummer calm near Batiscan.

the cottage to the ship's cabin. If you are lucky enough
to float around them in a canoe on a summer's evening
in Tadoussac or some other tiny port, you will get
glimpses of strong, easy-going men and bright-eyed,
buxom girls, hanging over the square stern in leisurely
content, perhaps singing some old sweet chanson to the
accompaniment of the indefatigable fiddle.

After we leave Eternity Bay and the Capes, we get
a glimpse of Trinity Bay on the north shore. We still
have thirty miles to go to reach Tadoussac. Presently
the river opens into a deep and beautiful Bay with a
picturesque village, steeped in peace and passiveness.
This is Anse St. Jean, at whose dock the steamers always
call.

Beyond Anse St. Jean we come upon the splendor
of the Little Saguenay. "Little" Saguenay! Yet this
wild stream that only hints at its allurements in the
beautiful valley seen from the river, is second only in
superb scenery to the Saguenay itself. Here is another
road back into the eternal Laurentians, with still more
silver streams and green robed hills, where summer plays
lonesomely for want of adventurers.

Here again is one of the imposing Saguenay views,
where the hills and the river curves blend into a great
picture of inspiring rhythms. Down stream the river

201

narrows and here stands Isle St. Louis. As we pass the island there is a great view ahead with Cape Sainte Marguerite towering against the eastern sky. On the right is a tiny "anse" with a timber mill and slender black stacks, a homely, cheerful human touch in all this imposing landscape. There are also piles of golden, scented pine planks waiting on the shore for the river schooners.

The Sainte Marguerite River, whose mouth is seen as we go farther down, is famous for its fish, while on the south shore next comes in view the rounded crest of Cape Crêpe, with beyond it Passe Pièrre, the deepest spot in the Saguenay.

On the north shore is seen the ball-like La Boule, nearly fifteen hundred feet high, which has given shelter to many a storm-bound vessel. It was behind La Boule that the French supply ships hid when they heard that Sir William Phipps from New England had gone up to lay seige to Quebec in 1690.

La Boule is one of the places that confirm my own personal belief that the Saguenay must have had its share of ear-ringed, cutlassed pirates. Certainly if I had been a pirate, sweeping the Spanish Main, I would have considered the Saguenay just the place for a treasure-hiding holiday. I would have brought my brass bound chests, full to the brim with old jewels, from

202

rings to coronets, and gem-encrusted chalices and blazing crosses, up to the legend-guarded Saguenay, and dropped anchor behind La Boule, while I searched about to select the perfect hiding place, in some gloomy cave or in a loam-filled pocket of rock. And when at last we had tired of scuttling Spanish treasure ships, back to the Saguenay my men and I would come, and spread the glittering jewels in the sun to watch the myriad lights flame from blood-red rubies, from emeralds rudely cut, from diamonds that once had hung about the warm white throats of young beauties, and there we would share our loot in leisure and in great content.

We are coming now close to Tadoussac. On the north shore we pass Barque Cove, and Anse a l'Eau, with its Government dock where the ferry from Rivière du Loup calls every day. There, too, is the Government Fish Hatchery which has distributed millions of salmon fry every year since it was built in 1875.

And so at last we are back at old, familiar Tadoussac, where the villagers, permanent and temporary, are at the dock to meet the boat. It is so easy to fall into the habit of meeting the boat, until it comes to feel like a daily responsibility. If you, too, have joined the curious crowds there, you can imagine the joy with which the

203

old traders went down to meet the spring ships from that far away European world they had left behind.

. . . .

Reluctantly we steam away again while the gulls swirl and dip over the wake of the vessel as it turns away from the royal Saguenay. We watch it as it recedes slowly into a last unforgetable picture, its giant hills silhouetted against the northern sky in a rhythm of symphonic beauty, faintly accented by the notations of color as they fade and blend, hill top beyond hill top. The Saguenay is now no longer a river of mystery. Beyond its granite portals lies a stream of imperishable memories.

Some day, staring wearily at a brick wall across a noisy street, or trying vainly to read, "Dear Sir, your letter of the nineteenth . . . ", suddenly they will fade away, and before your bewitched eyes you will see a rocky cliff, grey and green, russet and ochre, with bristling pine trees in its crown and a shimmering river at its feet, and in your ears will beat the music of the word Saguenay . . . ! Saguenay . . . ! Saguenay!